Beyond the Battle Line

The Korean War and My Life

By Luke Kim, M.D., Ph.D.

The cover photo is the North Korean refugees waiting to get aboard the U.S. ship at the Hungnam Harbor, North Korea, Dec. 1950.

Copyright © 2012 by Luke Kim, M.D., Ph.D.

Library of Congress Control Number:		2011918748
ISBN:	Hardcover	978-1-4653-5219-4
	Softcover	978-1-4653-5218-7
	Ebook	978-1-4653-5220-0

This book was printed in the United States of America.

To order additional copies of this book, contact:
Xlibris Corporation
1-888-795-4274
www.Xlibris.com
Orders@Xlibris.com
100859

CONTENTS

Preface By Luke Ik-Chang Kim, MD, Ph.D. 11

Foreword By Suk Choo Chang, M.D. 15

Foreword By Kay Chun, MSW, LCSW 19

Chapter 1. Where Did I Come From? 23
1-1 My origin and identity 23
1-2 Paternal grandfather Young Ho Kim
       and grandmother Young Hwa Kim: 25

       [1-2 A] Young Ho Kim, my paternal grandfather 25
       [1-2 B] Young Hwa Kim, Paternal grandmother........................ 27

1-3 My maternal grandfather Ha Ryung Choo and
       grandmother Nak Kyung Kim: 28

       [1-3 A] Ha Ryung Choo, my maternal grandfather 28
       [1-3 B] Nak Kyung Kim, my maternal grandmother..................29

1-4 My Parents Kwon Zik Kim and Woon Bong Choo:...........................31

       [1-4 A] Kwon Zik Kim, my father..31
       [1-4 B] Woon Bong Choo, my mother.....................................35

Chapter 2. The Developmental Years of My Life (1930-1949)......... 39
2-1 American missionaries' influence in the northern part of Korea.....39
2-2 Father's going to Japan for higher education...............................40
2-3 Kindergarten in Tokyo, Japan 41
2-4 Going to Yong-byon in North Korea..43

2-5 Transfer back to Sinuiju..45

2-6 Change from Korean name to Japanese name.....................46

2-7 Reverend Han Kyung Jik and his church.........................47

2-8 Cho Man Shik as the head of the
temporary national government.......................................48

2-9 Osan Middle School...49

2-10 Japan's general mobilization order for
Korean students to hard labor...52

2-11 News at the weapons factory of the
end of WWII on August 15, 1945...................................53

2-12 Return to Osan Middle School.......................................54

2-13 My first encounter with Soviet (Russian) soldiers.............55

2-14 Kim IL Sung as head of Communist North Korea............56

2-15 The Sinuiju student uprising incident.............................57

2-16 Modern exodus from North Korea..................................59

2-17 Father's escape from North Korea to
South Korea by fishing boat..59

2-18 My father's diary on his escape by the sea........................60

2-19 The rest of the family escaping to
South Korea through the 38th Parallel.............................60

2-20 Our life in Seoul prior to the Korean War.......................62

2-21 Family activities..63

2-22 My experiences at Seoul High School..............................64

Chapter 3 Korean War (1950-1953) **72**

3-1 Pre-Korean War geopolitical situation of Korea................72

3-2 Invasion of South Korea by the
North Korean People's Army...73

3-3 My "hiding place" and the kidnapping of my mother.........75

3-4 Escape to Buyo...77

3-5 My service as an interpreter in the
ROK Army Intelligence Unit..78

3-6 Involvement of the Chinese "Volunteer" Army.................79

3-7 Hungnam Evacuation...80

3-8 Dr. Bonghak Hyun's crucial role on rescuing NK refugees 82

3-9 My serving as a transport ship captain's interpreter 83

3-10 The Ship of Miracles: 84

3-11 R.J. McHatton, video producer 86

3-12 Impact of Hungnam Evacuation on my life 87

Chapter 4 Refugee Life In Busan (1951-1953) **89**

4-1 My return to Seoul and our family's train
     ride on the roof top to Busan 89
4-2 Our refugee life at the Yongdo Buddhist
     Temple refugee camp, Busan 91
4-3 My enlisting with the Korean Navy 91
4-4 Discharge from the military to go back to medical school..........93
4-5 My summer job as a secretary/interpreter with the Joint
     International Red Cross Team 95

Chapter 5 Family Life after the Korean War (1953-1962) **100**

5-1 Meeting Miss Chun Kyung Ja (전경자,田敬子), my future wife 100
5-2 Family Members 103
5-3 New stepmother Kim Young Ja (김영자, 金英子) 103
5-4 My social activities in Seoul 104
5-5 My siblings: 106

   [5-5 A] My sister Ik Nan Kim (김익란, 金益蘭) 106
   [5-5 B] Younger brother, Ik Sung Kim (김익성, 金益成)........111
   [5-5 C] Youngest brother, Ik Poong (Paul, 김익풍, 金益豊).....111

**Chapter 6. My Life in the US as a Graduate Student, Married Man
   and a First Generation Immigrant Asian American Psychiatrist
   (1956 to present)**.. **116**

6-1 Going to the US with two hundred dollars in my pocket 116
6-2 Rotating medical internship and graduate study
     in Clinical Psychology at University of Arizona 117
6-3 Colloquial English...118
6-4 Six years separation from Grace and one telephone call 120
6-5 Grace's encounter with orphaned teenagers: 120
6-6 Our wedding in Buffalo, New York 126
6-7 Ms. Jeannette Thompson as our "Godmother" 128
6-8 Driving my 59 Chevy from Buffalo to
     Vacaville, California across the country 130
6-9 Another medical internship in California: 131
6-10 My prison psychiatrist days at Vacaville Medical Facility 135
6-11 Contributions to the psychiatric profession and UC Davis........136
6-12 Introducing Korean Ethos....................................137

6-13   Contributions to the American Psychiatric Association (APA)
        and Association of Korean American Psychiatrists (AKAP).......140
6-14   Cultural psychiatry...146
6-15   Our lives dedicated to community service.....................147
6-16   Supporting "Worthy Causes of Education
        Toward Enlightenment"...147
6-17   Brief comments about Grace.....................................154
6-18   Our children and grandchildren...............................159

        [6-18 A] David Sung Chul Kim (김성철, 金聖喆)...................159
        [6-18 B] Daniel Sungwoo Kim (김성우, 金聖宇) 161

6-19   My life philosophy and bridge role
        between the East and West......................................164
6-20   Final Word...168

Reference **171**

Pictures **172**

Appendix **193**
1.   APA Psychiatric News Article on Dr. Luke Kim
        by Reporter Eva Bender...193
2.   Curriculum Vitae of Luke Ik-Chang Kim.....................198
3.   C.V. of Grace Sangok Kim 208
4.   Samples of my father Kwon Zik Kim's memoir
        note, writings and drawings for his grandchildren 213
5.   Korea and Korean People 219

        [5 A]   Contemporary Collective Experience of Koreans...........220
        [5 B]   The history of Korean immigration
                to the United States 221
        [5 C]   The First Wave 221
        [5 D]   The Second Wave...222
        [5 E]   The Third Wave 223

6. Korean Ethos..224
7. East and West Difference.......................................247
8. Therapeutic approach of Jeong-based relationships...................249
9. Association of Korean American Psychiatrists
    (AKAP) Activities..251

    [9 A] Paper presented on October 8, 1994 at AKAP
            California Society in LA...............................251
        [9 B] Newsletter article on Psychiatry and Spirituality
            on March 14, 2000 252

10. The CAPITAL and CAPITAL Foundation's
    Luke and Grace Kim "Profiles of Courage" Award...................253
11. Presbyterian Church Award for Grace Kim............................256
12. *Article on Ethnic Concerns Committee*............................258
13. California Governor Ronald Reagan's letter
    of commendation..268

THIS BOOK IS DEDICATED TO:

My father Mr. Kwon Zik Kim who guided me with his life philosophy and the Korean traditional culture and values.

My mother Woon Bong Choo, who was kidnaped by North Korean agents on August 28, 1950 during the Korean War and from whom we have not heard ever since. She was a community activist and a leader in Christian Women's organizations.

And my wife Grace Kim who has shared with me the same life goal and philosophy with her pure and abiding love.

Preface

By Luke Ik-Chang Kim, MD, Ph.D.

The year 2010 marked the 60th Anniversary of the Korean War, a tragic war which killed millions of civilians as well as military personnel on both sides, producing so many orphans and destroying and burning Seoul and other parts of South Korea to ashes. Following the ceasefire of the Korean War, the so-called 6-25 Conflict, more than half a century has passed, and yet the conflict between the North and South remains unsolved, and hostility with a threat of war still exists. I still get nightmares whenever I think about the Korean War.

Publisher Mr. Seung Tae Kim of Jeyoung Communications in Seoul, Korea, asked me to write and submit for publication my experiences of the Korean War, especially the marine evacuation operation from Hungnam Harbor, the so-called "Hungnam Evacuation" in which I was involved. I submitted my draft manuscript which included some of my life story. After reviewing it, the publisher felt that my life story would provide more meaningful context, and said that he preferred to publish the book as an autobiography rather than limiting the book to my Korean War experience. Thus, my autobiography in Korean was published in October 2010.

Over the span of the first 25 years of my life, I witnessed and passed through an epochal panorama of successive, abrupt and turbulent changes in Korea from one system of government to another with conflicting and opposite political ideologies, and then political revolutions and two wars!

The abrupt, drastic changes in modern Korea resulted particularly from the Japanese occupation of Korea with its colonial policy and the Communist government run by Kim IL Sung, from which we escaped to South Korea, a democratically oriented country. And then the Korean War broke out. These turbulent roller-coaster events impacted my life profoundly. I was totally unprepared for what was going on. I was frightened, confused, bewildered and demoralized.

However, I survived and eventually became stronger. It required a strong faith in God, courage, determination, perseverance, hope, sacrificial love of family members for each other, love of freedom and the will for survival. The most important source empowering my strength and determination has been my wife Grace with her abiding love, care and concern for me after our marriage in 1962. I must also mention the role of classical music, especially Bach and Beethoven, which helped me grow spiritually when I was feeling discouraged or depressed.

Originally I was thinking of writing a brief memoir for only my offspring. Then while expanding on my original manuscript, I wanted to share my life stories and experiences with more people, especially with the younger generations of Korean/Asian Americans who are not familiar with my generation's experiences. I feel that our generation is the last link to what I consider the most turbulent geopolitical period of time in modern history. The politically influential people in today's Korean society were born after the Korean War was over. Therefore, even these leaders are unfamiliar with what our generation went through with hardship. I want to share how we coped, survived, overcame adversities, and became stronger.

Many young second generation Korean Americans, including our own two sons have asked me to publish the book in English because they cannot read the Korean language. Thus this English version of my autobiography is being written and will be published soon. The English edition is not an exact translation of the original Korean edition. I have revised the contents quite freely.

The Korean version covered a brief introduction of my family background and my experiences during middle and high school days. In the English version, out of my respect and homage toward my ancestors, I will begin with the considerable pages devoted to the description of my grandparents and parents, especially the writings of my father so that such coverage may enlighten Korean/Asian second generation in appreciating the historical background of the Korean traditional values and Korean family system.

In both Korean and English versions, the main portion is devoted to the life experiences under the abrupt, successive political/social changes in Korea during pre- and post-World War II periods. This period included the hardships under the Japanese colonial occupation of Korea (1910-1945), the arbitrary division of Korea into North and South Korea at the convenience of Super-powers at the end of World War II (WWII), our life under the North Korean Stalinist-style Communist government, and our escape from North Korea to South Korea by crossing the 38th parallel. The book also covers my experiences during the Korean War (1950-53) itself, including the kidnaping of my mother by North Korean secret agents and the massive Hungnam Evacuation by the sea in which I participated. This was followed by my life in the United States as a graduate student at first (1956-60), and then afterward as a first generation immigrant Korean American psychiatrist, plus my wife Grace's experiences as a high school teacher in the United States.

I would like to thank several people who helped me tremendously in writing the book in Korean as well as writing the English version. My wife Grace has been especially instrumental in coordinating the entire publication process. In writing the Korean version, I had experienced limitations in typing and some memory problems due to my Parkinson's disease. Our good friend, Dr. Eui Young Yu, Professor Emeritus of Sociology at California State University (CSU) Los Angeles, played an indispensable role with his daily visits to our home, asking me appropriate questions to recall certain events and typing it in Korean. In this way, he contributed significantly in the completion of the Korean manuscript. Also, my sister-in-law Kay Chun, and my youngest brother Paul Kim reviewed the Korean language draft and made useful editorial suggestions.

For the English version of this book, I am very grateful to Ms. Shirley Roberts, a former English high school teacher and retired professor from California State University Long Beach for editing my English sentences, correcting grammatical errors and improving sentences. I would like to thank Mr. Tae Hyung Ji, a graduate student at California State University Long Beach, Miss, Michelle S. Lee, an undergraduate student at California State University Long Beach for their excellent knowledge and skill in computer, who helped me greatly with typing and organizing of the materials. Also I want to acknowledge the contribution of Jeffrey Thomas, English and communication teacher, for his last minutes inspection on my manuscript.

Finally, I am particularly thankful to Ms. Pattie Fong, editor of the API community newspaper Currents and attorney, for her diligent and hard work in taking overall charge of reviewing and editing of the entire English language draft.

Luke I.C. Kim MD, Ph.D.
Retired Clinical Professor of Psychiatry
University of California Davis School of Medicine
Now retired in Seal Beach Leisure World
Southern California, U.S.A.

Korean version of Luke's autobiography
Published in Korea, October, 2010

Foreword

Suk Choo Chang, M.D.

The autobiographical work by Luke Ik-Chang Kim describes his life throughout the turbulent 20th and into the 21st century in Korea, Japan and the United States. The book is modest in size, but rich in content. It can be divided into three periods: early life in northernmost Korea until age 15, the second period in Seoul where he experienced the Korean War, then his coming to America at age 26 in 1956.

Let me highlight one or two scenes from each period. Perhaps the most important event in his family history is the introduction to Christianity beginning with his maternal grandfather. It is interesting to speculate how the religion prospered in such a remote and landlocked area (speaking from this commentator's perspective of one who lived all his life in Seoul). The question is a part of a still larger question: why did it flourish in Korea, when it did not in either Japan or China? He nostalgically remembers blooming azalea in the front yard of his house on the hill. The flower, it seems, touched Korean ethos. Then his attendance at Osan Middle School. I knew it was an interesting school, but did not realize that it produced so many Koreans who contributed so much to Korean culture through art, literature and scholarship.

All those years were in the time of the Japanese occupation. During the occupation, one colonial policy that showed the bankruptcy of Japanese colonial cultural policy was the forcing of Japanese names on Koreans to whom the family name is almost sacred (1940). Then came the end of World War II (WWII,) the Japanese surrender, the division of Korea and the Kim family's escape to South Korea in 1945. The period between Korean liberation and the Korean War (1945-1950) was a most chaotic time for him, also for me. So many political parties, so much cacophony. The imposed division of Korea was an unknown invitation to the Korean War. Koreans more than most, have such a strong affinity among themselves which can be partly explained by the concept of *Jeong* as Luke came to emphasize years later. The Korean War was the most brutal and destructive war in the over three thousand years of Korean history because before there never were so many destructive weapons and a fratricidal war can be worse than any other. So Korea was literally razed from one end to the other. During the period the march of the U.N. forces to northernmost Korea and the retreat and evacuation, perhaps a best known part of the war, has been adequately described elsewhere. Only one thing should be noted. Luke played a significant part in helping so many refugees because the U.N. forces could not otherwise communicate with those hungry and frightened refugees shivering in the bitter cold. In this endeavor, as Luke mentions, Dr. Hyun Bonghak also played a pivotal role. He is the man with whom my wife and I traveled to China, Manchuria and Yeongil in 1978 shortly after the Nixon-Kissinger opening of the country.

Then the third period (1953). Luke Kim entered Seoul National University (SNU) Medical School and came to know Professor Nam Myungsuk, professor of psychiatry and the Psychiatry Department chairman. Who urged him to study clinical psychology, after which he was invited to work with him. Luke studied according to the mutually agreed plan. He completed a PhD in clinical psychology at University of Arizona in Tucson, Arizona, in 1960, and went into a psychiatric residency program in Buffalo, New York. However, by the time he was ready to return to Korea following his completion of all the necessary training, the professor passed away and Luke abandoned the plan. Instead he became a research director at a well-known forensic and correctional institution in California, and also became a clinical professor at UC Davis Medical School. Through his works there, he made many achievements and authored outstanding publications.

After retirement, Luke and Grace moved from Davis to Southern California to be near their family members, relatives and many old friends. They downsized their lifestyle by selling their Davis house where they had lived for 36 years and buying a 1,000 square foot house in Seal Beach Leisure World. Most recently they (Luke and Grace) donated to the Department of Psychiatry, University of California Davis School of Medicine all of the leftover money from the sale of the Davis house minus the purchase of the house in Leisure World and their moving expenses in order to create the Luke and Grace Endowed Professorship in Cultural Psychiatry. After a three year nationwide search, a well-known cultural psychiatrist, Francis Lu, MD was recruited to the position of the Luke & Grace Kim Endowed Professorship. Following their retirement to Seal Beach in Orange County, they continue to serve actively in the community.

The above describes only half of his adult life because there was always a better half right beside him, his wife Grace Kim (or Miss Chun Kyung Ja). They first met during the war in Busan (previously Pusan) through student Christian activities and their relationship continued in Seoul after returning there. After Luke came to America they continued their relationship through weekly love letters for six years and they finally married in Buffalo, New York in 1962. Since then Grace has been always behind, beside or before him, devoting much of her time in community and social activities to bring people together and to help them, for which she has been given many awards and acknowledgement, so much so that the above mentioned professorship is in their joint names. She has magnetism and charisma. Grace has been more than a better half.

Like "*a small boat in the rough sea of 20th century Korea and beyond,*" in finishing my brief reflection on their life stories, my summary sense tells me their lives have been where somehow they fit in so naturally, resiliently and snugly. And my wife and I are fortunate to have known them for so many years. In editing such a work I also appreciate the valuable support provided by Professor Eui-Young Yu.

Suk Choo Chang, M.D.
Retired Clinical Professor of Psychiatry, Yale Medical School
Now retired in Seattle, Washington

Foreword

By Kay Chun, MSW, LCSW

My first memory of meeting Luke is when I was about five or six years old when he started dating Grace, my older sister, whom he later married, so I have known him practically all my life. I consider it a blessing to have been part of his life and bear witness to his life's journey, an "epic poem" if you will, filled with valiant struggles, courage, endurance, and achievements, often exemplifying love and compassion. Luke's gifts, contributions, and accomplishments are many and they bestride the professional and personal realms—an esteemed psychologist, psychiatrist, educator, community activist, and a loving family man. Luke has embraced and transcended impressively the pain and the suffering of his past experiences—the childhood and young adult years filled with hardships and losses, all resulting from the two major tragic historical turbulences and their horrendous impacts: the Japanese occupation and the Korean War. The command of his empathetic mind seems to be rooted in the fact that he himself has overcome the entrapment of suffering.

His often-heard spontaneous and considerate inquiry, "How can I be of help?" must come from the "heart-mind place" that embraces both qualities of the devotional heart and reflective insights. When he is involved in helping others or tackling social justice issues, you can feel his passion, focused attention, and commitment. He seems to have unwavering trust in the Divine Will and it is this trust that fuels his soul-driven pursuit for his fellow human beings' welfare even in the face of obstacles or disappointments.

Reading his biographical sketches in the following pages is a journey in itself. Many contours of an epoch are compressed into Luke's personalized life story. It provides a delightful backstage tour of the tumultuous events of the twentieth-century Korea as they were lived through one courageous man, who later overcame the challenges of an immigrant life and turned those challenges into a success story of achievements and contributions. It is the story of a man whose journey of resolute will and unswerving trust is a witness to the spirit of a triumphant soul.

Kay Chun, MSW, LCSW
The Strasmki Developmental Assessment Center
Long Beach Memorial Medical Center
Long Beach, California
May, 2011

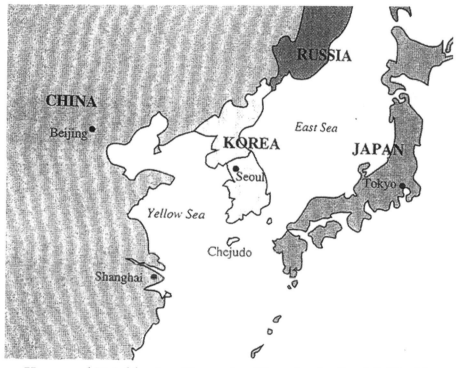

Korea and Neighboring Countries (Drawing by Patrick Hurh)

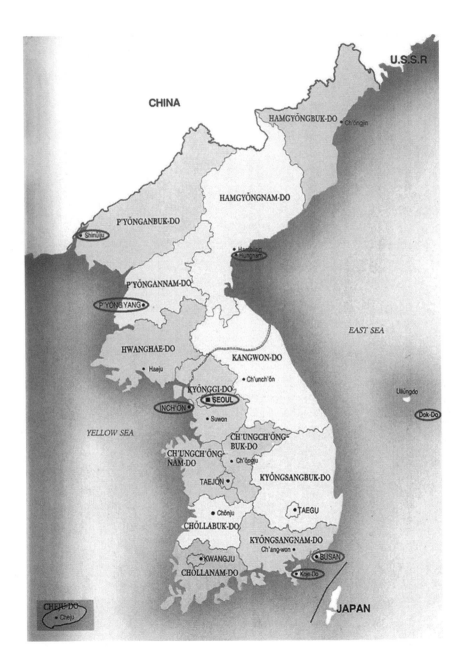

Chapter 1.

Where Did I Come From?

My origin, grandparents and parents:

[1-1] My origin and identity: My full name is Luke Ik-Chang Kim (Luke,김익창,金益昌). I was born on April 22, 1930 in Sinuiju as the eldest son of four children (three sons and one daughter) of Korean parents. Sinuiju is the capital city of P'yonganbuk-Do Province in currently North Korea and is a small to medium size harbor city located in the far northwestern region of North Korea along the Yalu River, which borders with China. When I was born, Korea had long been declared a Japanese protectorate (1905) and annexed by Japan (1910).

When I was five, I attended Ikebukuro Kindergarten in Toyko. I was 7 years old when I went to Yong-byon Elementary School in North Korea. Three years later, we returned to Sinuiji and I attended Wakadake Elementary School. At age 12, I was accepted and attended Osan Middle School in Jung-Ju. At age 15, my entire 9th grade class was forced to work at an ammunitions factory in P'yongyang (North Korea) until the end of World War II on August 15, 1945. After the war, I transferred to Dong-Joong Middle School in Sinuiju to be with my family. In June 1946, the family fled to South Korea and I entered Seoul High School. In 1949 I graduated from Seoul High School and began my studies at Seoul National University as a premed student. On June 25, 1950 the North

Korean Army invaded South Korea, and captured Seoul in 3 days. My mother was kidnapped on August 28, 1950, and my two younger brothers and I fled to Buyo. After return to Seoul from Buyo, I joined and served as a non-commissioned interpreter's position in the Republic of Korea (ROK) Army Intelligence Unit, participating in the Hungnam Evacuation during the Korean War. Then I returned to Busan and enlisted in the Korean Navy and was later transferred to the Korean Marine Corps. The military terminated my enlistment so that I could enter and finish medical school. In 1956, I graduated from Seoul National University Medical School, with an M.D. degree.

On June 5, 1956, I left Busan for the United States on a student visa traveling by Korean cargo ship, and arrived at Newport, Oregon, two weeks later. Following one year of rotating medical internship in Tucson, AR, I enrolled at the University of Arizona as a graduate student and received my Ph.D. in clinical psychology in July 1,1960. After completing one year of clinical psychology intern at Buffalo, and then I started my training on the psychiatric residency program at Buffalo, NY, and completed the psychiatric resident program at Napa CA, which made me to be eligible for certification by the Psychiatric specialty board. I married Miss Sang Ok Chun in May 12, 1962, at the Buffalo Presbyterian Church in Buffalo, New York officiated by Rev. John E. Woods. On January 2, 1968, I became a naturalized United States citizen in San Francisco, and adopted "Luke" as the additional first legal name. Thus my full name became: *Luke* Ik-Chang Kim. My wife adopted "Grace" as her additional first legal name, so she became: *Grace* Sang-Ok Kim.

At present I am 81 years old, 5.5 feet tall, and weigh 125 pounds. I was diagnosed as having Parkinson's disease about eight years ago, which changed my life style and brings new challenges every day. I do not have tremors of hands, but I do have symptoms of slow, shuffling gait, unsteady walking with frequent falls, weak and soft voice with speech difficulties, and "Micrographia", involuntary tendency to write smaller and smaller letters to the point where I cannot read my own letters myself. There are no basic treatments that cure Parkinson's disease, but I am continuing diligently the supportive medications, exercise, physical therapy, and speech therapy. Currently, my wife Grace Sang-Ok and I reside in a retirement community in Seal Beach California which provides many activities, clubs and an abundance of friends.

Luke I.C. Kim

[1-2] Paternal grandfather Young Ho Kim and grandmother Young Hwa Kim:

[1-2 A] Young Ho Kim, my paternal grandfather,

was born on June 1, 1876 in Uiju, P'yonganbuk-Do Province in currently North Korea, and passed away on March 11, 1931, at age 55, when I was only one year old. I have no memory of him except seeing him in the only available family photo (see the photo below). He was a descendant of "Kyung Ju" Kim, whose ancestor was a king during the Shilla Dynasty (4th-6th Century A.D.) At age 14, he was baptized by an American missionary and became a devout Christian member of the Presbyterian Church.

Grandfather Kim was a "scholar" and practiced herbal medicine and acupuncture. He was a "home" (informal) teacher of Chinese classics. Informal homeroom teaching was called "*Suh-dang*" in Korean in the old days. (see photo below). There were no public schools and he taught a small group in his home paid for by students bringing rice, or some chicken; as there was no formal tuition.

This is the only photo that includes my paternal grandfather Young Ho Kim and the baby is the author. Front left is grandfather, right is grandmother, standing behind is my mother on the left, my father, baby Luke Kim, and aunt.

Homeroom teaching at Suh-dang

The family was from the northwest corner of Korea—the town of Uiju, just south of the Yalu River which is the border between Korea and Manchuria. According to my father who at times accompanied grandfather and watched him work, Grandfather Kim traveled to Manchuria occasionally to administer acupuncture treatment and herbal medicine and would stay with the sick person's family for several days. Grandfather was described as a gentle, honest, hard-working man.

[1-2B] Young Hwa Kim, my paternal grandmother,

was born in 1875 at Uiju and passed away in 1961, at the age of 86 poisoned by gas fumes of briquettes burning during the night. She was bent forward markedly in her posture due to heavy farm work, and she appeared to be uncomfortable most of the time.

The family name "Kim" has several subgroups traceable to different ancient places of origin. I heard that my grandmother was from the "Kim Hae" Kim lineage, while grandfather is from the "Kyung Ju" Kim royal ancestral line. Grandmother came from the well-to-do *yang ban* (ruling class), and her family owned quite a bit of farmland. Grandfather's side was not as rich or high class as grandmother's side was.

Grandfather Kim came from the family background that, although they were poor, emphasized studying and more scholastic or educational achievements. That background is in keeping with the idea that he studied herbal medicine.

Grandmother used to carry paper-wrapped candies all the time in a large pocket of her Korean style underwear, "long Johns," beneath her skirt. Long before our marriage, Grace used to visit me at our home in Seoul. During Grace's visit, grandmother would say "Would you like some candies?" and gave candies to Grace from her pocket many times. Grace also remembers that Grandmother Kim used to touch Grace's ear lobes and say that Grace had plum-like ear lobes which are "*bok gui*" (= blessed ear lobes) meaning she will have good fortune and a happy life without worrying about an empty stomach. It is too bad that Grandmother Kim died from coal briquette coal (carbon monoxide) gas poisoning.

My paternal grandmother Young Hwa Kim

[1-3] My maternal grandfather Ha Ryung Choo and grandmother Nak Kyung Kim:

[1-3 A] Ha Ryung Choo, my maternal grandfather,

was born in North Korea in March, 1885 and passed away in 1942 in Seoul. I have no memory of him whatsoever because I never met him, nor did we ever have an opportunity to visit due to the far distance between his residence in Seoul and ours far north in Sinuiju. He graduated from P'yongyang Presbyterian Seminary in 1922 (12th graduating class) and was ordained as a Presbyterian minister with his first ministry serving Joongkangjin Presbyterian Church in North Korea for 10 years and later at Yang-Pyong-Dong Church in Yungdeung-Po, Seoul until he passed away in 1942.

I heard that Reverend Choo participated in the March First Independence Movement and was arrested for his involvement in that protest. He was put in prison for one year where he became very physically weak. He passed away in 1942 at a relatively young age of 57.

My maternal grandfather Ha Ryung Choo

I did not know much about Reverend Choo until I started writing this book. In my computer-search for information on him, I found published articles that reported he was indeed a brave patriot involved in the nationwide demonstration called the 1919 March 1st Korean Independence Movement. A Korean newspaper Hankook Il-Bo on April 4, 2004 published an article "Kang-Ge Massacre": "On April 8, 1919, a Japanese military police platoon shot and killed mercilessly two hundred Koreans crowded in the street market shouting for Korean independence from the Japanese colonial occupation." The newspaper further documented events leading up to the Kang-Ge Massacre: "A seminary student, Mr. Ha Ryung Choo, who at the time happened to be in Seoul, found a marching crowd there in Seoul streets distributing the flyers of the Korean Independence declaration. He took a copy of the flyer with him and went to his hometown, Kang-Ge (located currently in North Korea). There in his hometown, together with his friends, he mobilized a large crowd in the street market on a market day, and read the document of the Korean Independence Declaration. Then the crowd began marching on the street shouting 'Korean Independence!' A Japanese military police (MP) platoon showed up and began to spray bullets into the crowd blindly, killing about two hundred Koreans and injuring scores of people." I must say that as a result of my recent discovery of the brave patriotism of my grandfather, Reverend Choo, I began to feel very proud of him and have a high respect for him.

I would like to introduce an interesting episode about Reverend Choo. I heard this story from my mother. Reverend Choo was giving a sermon at Sae-Moon-Ahn Presbyterian Church in Seoul and was wearing traditional Korean style man's *hanbok* which has baggy trousers with a silky waistband, but without belt stoppers (belt loops). In the middle of the sermon, his silk baggy trousers suddenly dropped to the floor. So he promptly told the parishioners in the middle of his sermon "Let us pray!" While people bowed their heads praying, he was able to pull the trousers back up to his waist. It is easy for a man to wriggle and move his body around causing *hanbok* silk trousers to slip down to the floor when there are no belt stoppers.

[1-3 B] Nak Kyung Kim, my maternal grandmother,

was born in 1890 at Kang-Ke, P'yonganbuk-Do Province, North Korea and passed away in January, 1951 at age 61 in Seoul during the Korean War. Kang-Ke is noted as the birthplace of beautiful Korean women, who are taller than average Korean women and have light, porcelain skin. Both my maternal grandmother and Grace's grandmother were born in Kang-Ke, and both were beautiful, tall, and fair skinned.

We knew our maternal grandmother pretty well because when our family escaped to Seoul from North Korea, we lived together under the same roof for one year and a half. With my uncle Daebyuk Choo's hospitality, our family lived in a room of his two story Japanese style house in Seoul. While we were living in that house, Grandmother Kim was raising three orphaned grandchildren (two boys, Bong Duk and Neung Duk, and one girl, Ae Nah). They were the children of my two maternal uncles who died at relatively young ages. These uncles were graduates of Yonsei University which was founded by American missionaries. They were very fond of music. I heard that one uncle was very good on the saxophone and clarinet, and the other uncle was skilled on the trumpet. There was always music in the family. In both cases, their wives died first from tuberculosis (TB) of the lung, and then both uncles also died of tuberculosis. In those days, tuberculosis was the most common cause of death because then there was no effective medicine against the disease. One orphaned cousin, Bong Duk, and the girl, Ae Nah, are now mature grownups. The youngest boy Neung Duk disappeared during the Korean War. We do not know whether he is alive or dead, or whether he was kidnapped and taken to North Korea.

Grandmother Kim was tough and strict with her three orphaned grandchildren. I remember that grandmother would slap my cousins if they did not behave well or fought among themselves. I do not remember them ever having much time for fun. I felt sorry for Ae Nah, Bong Duk, and Neung Duk for having to deal with our tough, punitive grandmother. In spite of this strict upbringing, Ae Nah became a warm, sincere and beautiful lady who was a deacon at Youngnak Presbyterian Church in Korea, and currently lives in Seal Beach Leisure World where we live. Bong Duk worked for the Korean government in the intelligence field from which he retired and lives a comfortable life with his wife in Seoul, Korea.

[1-4] My Parents Kwon Zik Kim and Woon Bong Choo:

[1-4 A] Kwon Zik Kim, my father, was born on December 1, 1902, to Korean parents, Young Ho Kim and Young Hwa Kim, as the only son of six children (three older sisters and two younger sisters) in the town of Uiju, P'yonganbuk-Do Province, in current North Korea. He and his ancestral families have had only one son in each generation for four successive generations. My father was a gentle, quiet, soft-spoken, diligent, hard-working person. For the first ten years or so he worked with the prefecture government of P'yonganbuk-Do Province as a civil servant during the period of the Japanese occupation and for a brief period prior to his escape from North Korea at the end of WWII.

My father was a person who had a college education and worked as a civil engineer most of his life. He spent working for private construction companies in South Korea during second half of his life. In terms of his personality, he can be described as "gentle outside, but strong and determined inside." He was relatively non-verbal and task-oriented as seen in his deeds and actions. He was frequently absent from home due to his extended business trips as a civil Engineer.

When he returned home, he became a strict displinarian, and therefore he appeared to be an emotionally distant and fearful father to us when we were young. However, after my mother was kidnapped (about her being kidnapped, further details will be covered in the Chapter 2 subsection "My hiding place and the kidnapping of my mother"), he became much kinder, gentler, closer to us. He was working hard in taking care of his growing children, playing the both roles of father and mother.

Cultural Foot Note:

1. According to the Western/American system, if a female, for example, Miss Elizabeth *Chun*, married a man Steve *Lee*, she adopts and uses her husband's family name, like "Elisabeth *Lee*" and not her maiden name. However, in the Korean/Chinese system, even if a female married a man named Steve *Lee*, she retains her own Elizabeth maiden name *Chun*, and never becomes "Elizabeth *Lee*," using her husband's family name. That's why my maternal grandfather's name was Ha Ryung *Choo;* however, my grandmother's name was *Nak Kyung Kim*.

2. In the western/American tradition, when a full name is addressed, the given name comes first and then the family name comes last, like "Luke *Kim*." In the Korean/Asian tradition, the family name is in the first position and the given first name is in the second position, for example, "*Kim* Luke." It is confusing. In this book I will use the American system most of the time with the exception of several well-known persons who maintained the Korean/Asian name tradition, such as *Kim IL Sung, Mao* Tse Tung, *Chiang* Kai Shek, Rev. *Han* Kyung Jik, etc.

3. Among the Korean family names, Kim, Lee, and Park will occupy 45% of the entire Korean family names and the other 55% would be divided among 200 family names, usually single-word family names like Choi, Jung, Kang, Cho, and so forth.

4. In America, it is common to casually address or refer to a person by their given first name, such as "John," "David," and "Mary." However, in Korea, only the family name is used and spoken. First names are almost never used, and usually only by equal colleagues. Hierarchical societies, like Korea, utilize honorific language. Those above or below in status would address or refer to a person by their status, i.e., Teacher Kim, Elder Lee or Chairman Park. Koreans prefer formality in their salutations because doing so implies more respect.

    In English, the most equalitarian and convenient pronoun used is "you," because one can use "you" regardless of the social status of the person. "You" can be used to address to the U.S. President, your professor, your classmate, your wife, your younger sister, a slave, and even the dog. In Korean society, an intimate form of "you" ("*yobo*," "*dang shin*" which is equivalent to "honey") is reserved and used only in privacy between married couple and lovers. In Korean society more often, couples in front of people will refer to each other in an indirect manner as "David's father" and "David's mother." Usually the parent would use their oldest son's first name. Sometimes in the Korean culture, a wife would be referred to as the "inside person" and the husband as the "outside person."

From his young adult age, father kept writing a meticulous diary and memoir in his excellent penmanship. In fact while drafting this manuscript, I referred to his diary frequently to determine the exact dates of certain events during our childhood and growing years. Father had exceptional talent in calligraphy with brushes and black ink and wrote some well known Biblical quotations, such as Psalm 23, on scrolls in Chinese characters as well as in the Korean alphabet. Some of these scrolls have become treasures of our family, relatives and close friends.

The English translation of some early pages of his diary will be provided as follow.

For example, my father described his home environment in his diary, as follows: "There was a small mountain behind our house and I used to climb up to the mountain top which gave me a full view of the surroundings. Also, in front of the house there was a small creek, and along the creek there were five or six bushes producing blackberries. In the fall, blackberries would drop into the creek and I used to pick them out to eat those tasty blackberries."

He continued: "There was a small river not far from our house where I used to bathe and swim during the summer. Also, I remember that at one time during winter, I walked on the frozen icy river and the ice broke up causing me to fall into the water. The river was not deep but my clothes got wet and I returned home crying."

"In those days boys and girls had long braided ponytails with a red colored silk ribbon tied at the end. When a young man married, he wore his braid wrapped into a bun on top of his head, and then he covered the bun with a skull cap *"gahm-tu"* in Korean which had an extra bump to cover the bun. The *gahm-tu* was worn inside the house. However, when married men went outside the house, they wore a *"gaht"* (see the photo below), a black, wide brimmed hat covering the *gahm-tu*. The *gaht* had a high crown and was made out of horsetail hair.

The left side photo shows gahm-tu on the left, and gaht on the right. Right side photo shows gaht.

While inside the house, the *gaht* was removed, however "*gahm-tu*" skull cap still remains in the head"

"When I was eight years old, I went with my father to a small Korean Christian church where we heard an American missionary preaching on Jesus whom we had never heard of before. But there and then, we accepted Jesus, and became Christians. At that time we met a young American missionary couple who sang the hymn, "Must Jesus bear the cross alone, and all the world go free? . . . . there's a cross for me" which became one of my favorite hymns. The young missionaries appeared enviably a wonderful and noble couple. I still remember their appearance and singing voices."

"From eight years old on, I began to learn Chinese characters in order to study Chinese literature. For two years, I attended *suh-dang* (home-based learning place with one teaching instructor and a small number of students). We had to read Chinese characters out loud, and the louder I read, the better I became at memorizing. The instructor supervised, checking whether students were reading out loud or not. Usually the following day we had to recite phrases or a poem in Chinese characters in front of the teacher and students flawlessly from our memory. If we failed, we were whipped on the calf of the legs with a thin flexible bamboo stick. I got hit only once when students were making noises, but not for failure in memorizing Chinese characters. When the instructor went away from the room briefly, students used to stop reading aloud, and when he returned to the room, the students began to read loudly again."

"At 12 years old, the first photograph was taken of me. Also at Baeshin Elementary school, I saw a trumpet for the first time when all the students were gathered on the grounds for an all-day sports day. I saw a bicycle for the first time which an American missionary was riding on."

"When I was fifteen years old, I was baptized by an American missionary. When I became baptized, I had my long hair cut short, like a crew-cut, as a sign of my conversion to Christianity. When I returned home, my grandmother was surprised and upset about my new short haircut. She scolded me severely, telling me to get out of the house."

"In February, 1919, when I was 17 years old, I graduated from Baeshin Elementary School with honor. At that time elementary schools were an eight year system which consisted of four years of basic classes and four years of advanced classes. From a contemporary point of view, eight years of elementary school was too long, and a lot of wasted time."

"In March, 1919, an independence movement occurred among Korean people.

At that time several hundred people were gathered carrying the Korean National flag, *Taegukgi*, and shouting "*Dok-Lip-Man-se*!" (*Dok Lip* means Korean Independence, *mansei* means long life.)

"In 1922, I entered the well-known Soongshil Middle School in P'yongyang which was founded by American missionaries. In 1924, I was elected as the school's entire student body president. During the final term examination, our class demonstrated a 'strike' to protest against an incompetent teacher by boycotting answering the questions of his final examinations. For this incident, the school authority made me responsible for the strike, and expelled me from the school as a "sacrificial lamb" for the boycott event. To this day, I am resentful and disagree with the school's decision to expel me from the school, and thereby not be able to graduate from Soongshil Middle School."

"A Japanese military police hit me hard on my face and left ear, which caused a permanent hearing loss of my left ear."

"Our family moved to Manchuria (currently China). There, from April 1919 to February 1920, I served as secretary to the Korean Independence Fighter Party of the Ahnjigeu Branch in Manchuria which was associated with the Korean Provisional Government in exile in Shanghai, China. At that time, I met such notable, well-known Independence fighters, as Oh Dong Ji, Cho Ji Ha, Yoon Ha Young, and others."

[1-4 B] Woon Bong Choo, my mother, was born on November 8, 1904 in Kang-Ge, in P'yonganbuk-Do Province, in currently North Korea. She was kidnapped by North Korean secret agents on August 28, 1950 and we have not heard from her since. (Further details will be covered in the Chapter 3 subsection 3-3 "My hiding place and the kidnapping of my mother").

My mother was very sociable, fun-loving, and talented in music, literature, as well as competent community leader. She used to keep a diary and wrote poems which Grace and I happened to see once, but somehow her writings have disappeared and are not available now. Up until the 1950s, traditionally many Korean parents favored male over female in supporting their higher education. There was no equal opportunity for higher education between the two genders. In those old days, sending a daughter from a far distant province to the capital city of Seoul in order to give her an opportunity to attend high school was rare, but that is what my maternal grandparents did. My mother attended the Sookmyung Girls High School, an elite school in Seoul founded by the Korean Royal family.

My mother was an educated intelligentsia for that period. She was regarded as a *shin-yuh-sung* ("new educated woman") wearing a hat and trousers in western style. She was a women's leader. She had a lot of dreams for her life, but she did not have an opportunity to accomplish her aspirations as a "new educated woman" in those days. She met my father as both of them worked as civil servants at the Prefecture of P'yonganbuk-Do. And they got married to each other. She was living as a wife of a salaried civil service husband in Korea under Japanese occupation; their living standard was so-so at a middle class level for that period. Their life was not really comfortable because goods and food were tight and rationed in the WWII war effort that was becoming increasingly intensive. Because of her rather hard life and unfulfilled dreams, she was often frustrated. My mother was more socially active, outgoing, and fun-loving than my father was. Miss. Choi Seunghee, a world-famous Korean ballet dancer, used to come to Sinuiju occasionally to perform her unique and exquisite Korean solo dances. Although my mother was a few years older than Choi Seunghee, they were members of the alumni association of Sookmyung Girls High School. My mother used to organize a welcoming party for Choi Seunghee whenever she came to Sinuiju.

My mother was always interested in our education and chose the best schools for us to attend. I remember my mother suggesting to me that I should study medicine because I was one of the top students in the class and had good academic grades in math and science. She also expressed her hope for Ik Nan that she should be married to a medical doctor or study pharmacy herself. Both of us were obedient and obliged. Ik Nan began to study science subjects harder to prepare for the pharmacy school examination. I did choose medicine as my profession. However at the end Ik Nan chose fine arts for her studies.

My mother Miss Choo a student at Sookmyung Girls High School

Parent engagement photo on October 29, 1929 in Seoul

My Parent's wedding of western style at Samil Church in Sinuiju
on December 28. 1929

Wedding of my father and mother

My mother after first son Luke was born in 1930

Chapter 2.

The Developmental Years of My Life (1930-1949)

[2-1] American missionaries' influence in the northern part of Korea: At the turn of the 19th Century, many American missionaries visited the northern part of Korea spreading the gospel with the result of an increasing number of Koreans becoming Christians. John H. Heron, Horace N. Allen M.D., Horace Underwood, Henry Appenzeller and Samuel Moffet were the earliest missionaries who came to Korea between 1884 and 1889 and by 1890 they reached the remote northwest part of Korea.

It was reported that in 1889 Reverend Underwood baptized 33 Korean Christians in the Yalu River and that in 1891 the first Christian church was establish in Uiji. These missionaries contributed greatly to opening hospitals and establishing several medical schools and colleges, including Yonhee College by Horace Underwood and Ewha Women's College by Henry Appenzeller. Dr. Allen became the first Western physician appointed as a family doctor to the Royal family. In 1901, Moffet Samuel held small group meetings at his home, which became the beginning of the P'yongyang United Presbyterian Seminary. In 1907, the first seven Korean Presbyterian ministers graduated from that seminary. Thus, P'yongyang has been referred to as the Asian Jerusalem and P'yongyang became a center of

Christian activities throughout the northern part of Korea. My maternal grandfather Reverend Choo attended and graduated from P'yongyang United Presbyterian Seminary.

For Koreans, such contact with the western culture through these early pioneering missionaries planted seeds for the ideas of freedom, democratic principles, and independence. As a result, many people in the northern part of Korea became interested in seeking higher education including going abroad to Japan and the United States to study science and technology. Moreover, American missionaries encouraged Korean women to learn how to read *Hangul*, the Korean alphabet, so that they could read the Korean Bible. *Hangul* was created by scholars under the direction of King Sae Jong 500 years ago and it is the most scientific alphabet system. *Hangul* has 24 characters consisting of vowels and consonants and is very simple to learn and is written just as it is pronounced.

My paternal grandfather came into contact with American missionaries who encouraged him to become a Christian. Our families, including my grandchildren, comprise five generations of Presbyterian Christians. As a result of this introduction of Christianity into the northern part of Korea, Koreans came into contact with western culture, especially western technology, literature, and ideology.

[2-2] Father's Going to Japan for Higher Education: My father, who was the only son in the family, felt that
he had the responsibility of looking after the family and had the dream of obtaining a college degree in order to earn more and provide a more comfortable life. Father decided to go to Japan for advanced training even though he had married my mother in 1929 and already had three children. My father initially went to Japan alone, leaving his family behind in Korea for one and a half years. According to my father's diary, Grandfather Kim sold one of his house for 20 yen (a fairly large sum of money for Koreans at that time) and gave that money to father for the initial expenses of going to Japan to study. My father studied at the Tokyo Butsuri-Gakko (Tokyo Institute of Technology, equivalent to MIT in stature and reputation). However, he missed his family so much that he decided to bring the family—our mother and three children (myself—5 years old, my 3 year old younger sister and 1 year old younger brother)—to join him in Japan.

My mother and we three children took a train from Sinuiju to Busan (formerly Pusan) which were the two most distant end points of the railroad system covering Korea from north to south. While on the train, my mother taught me how to count in Japanese (1, 2, 3, 4 = *ichi, ni, san, shi*) as well as some other simple Japanese words. Following our arrival in Tokyo in September 1935, our family lived with my father in a private dormitory located in the Ikebukuro district of Tokyo. The dormitory was sponsored by a Christian foundation for Korean students studying in Japan.

Family photo at Tokyo in 1935. 2nd left is Luke, sister Ik Nan, and brother Ik Sung.

[2-3] Kindergarten in Tokyo Japan: I enrolled in
Ikebukuro Kindergarten in Tokyo. In kindergarten, the children were engaged in war games and they did not accept me as a member when I wanted to play with them in these popular war games. Instead my Japanese peers called me by derogatory words like "*chosen-jin* (a negative label of Koreans in Japanese)." Although I was very young, I learned that Koreans were discriminated against by some Japanese as an ethnic minority.

One day my mother and I went to the public bath. In those old days, many Japanese households did not have private bath/shower facilities and people went to public bath houses where they took a shower and bath in public. The hot water of the bath was too hot for me and the tender skin of my right toes became red and burned. I developed a high fever and swollen legs, was hospitalized and the doctor diagnosed me as suffering from septicemia. Apparently bacteria went into the burnt area and spread through the blood vessels throughout my entire body causing septicemia. At that time my father was working very hard in the daytime at an "*arbeit*" (student side job) and attending classes in the evening. He became physically exhausted and began to lose his health. He developed pneumonia and intercostal neuralgia requiring hospitalization. My father and I were hospitalized in the same room at the Ikebukuro hospital. It was too much for my father working day and night to study and support his family. The hospital expenses were more than 300 Yen, which totally broke him financially. At that point he decided to quit school and return to Korea before he could graduate from the university. Since then he had a lifelong deep "*haan*" (Korean word referring to feelings of regret, resentment, and unexpressed anger) for not being able to complete his college degree.

More than several times my father told me how much he regretted, feeling his life-long *haan*-ridden emotions, not being able to graduate twice, first from the Soongshil Middle School where he was expelled unfairly as a sacrificial lamb for the student protest, and later from the Tokyo Institute of Technology due to his physical illness and financial burdens. I took his advice to my heart and I have to make sure to complete whatever project I am doing.

My father had a dream of becoming a high school math/science teacher and/or college professor because he did not like his civil engineer job. It was demanding and required him to be away from home for extended periods. Moreover, as a head honcho of construction sites, he had to perform the duty of supervising local engineers and construction workers in major project sites including water irrigation dams, tunnels and highway roads. In his diary, my father expressed his discomfort and distaste as a sincere and dedicated practicing Christian working in the rough and tumble environment of construction. In that environment, there was a lot of drinking and undesirable activities, for instance, womanizing acts, profanity, bribery and other cheating at the construction sites themselves. When he refused to join the drinking parties, he was isolated and ostracized. That is why he hoped to change careers and wanted a teaching job. However, because he did not complete his college degree, he had no choice but to go back to his previous job as a civil engineer for P'yonganbuk-Do Province. This time, however, he was re-assigned and transferred to the Yong-byon branch office.

(Special communication to my Japanese-American friends)

I would like to say at this point that one of my best friends is Japanese, and that I have many wonderful splendid Japanese American friends. I totally differentiate between the policy operated by the Imperial Japanese Government in the early 20th Century and my Japanese American friends who are Untied States citizens and some of whom fought against the German /Japanese enemies as U.S. soldiers. Japanese Americans had nothing to do with the past Imperial Japanese Government. Therefore, the description of my early life experiences under the Japanese control of Korea should not offend nor cause any uncomfortable feelings to my many good Japanese American friends who are reading this book.

[2-4] Going to Yong-byon in North Korea: The

whole family moved to Yong-byon from Tokyo when I was seven years old. I remember how uneasy and disappointed I felt on that trip to Yong-byon. We had to ride a bus for two hours from the railroad station to the town of Yong-byon. The bus ride on an unpaved, dirt road was very rough and shook us up quite a bit. This was in contrast to the paved asphalt roads of Japan which made a car ride quiet and smooth. Also, the thatched roof houses along the road looked shabby and poor.

My father worked as a civil engineer at the Yong-byon branch office under a Japanese department head. Once we moved to Yong-byon, my parents became active members of Yong-byon Presbyterian Church. I remember that at Christmas time I played the role of one of the three wise men in the Christmas play. Our house was on a hill with a good view. In the front garden were azalea flowers in full bloom. My mother raised several brown-colored Korean native chickens. Once my younger brother Ik Sung went out to the front yard with a piece of rice on his lips. One of the chickens saw it and jumped into my brother's face in an attacking manner to pick that piece of rice off his upper lip; the chicken caused injury to Ik Sung's lips. Ik Sung is 76 years old now and still has the scar on his upper lip from that chicken's attack.

Yong-byon Elementary School was directed by a Japanese principal, but the majority of the teachers were Korean. Classes were taught in Japanese while we spoke Korean at home. At the elementary school, we once assembled for a whole school sports day. I remember there was a pretty girl who held my hand during the Korean circle dance and that made me happy. Our school went for a picnic on the Yaksan Mountains near Yong-byon and there were many huge pine trees. With my pocketknife, I carved my name "Kim Ik Chang" deeply into the trunk of one big pine tree. I thought I would go back some day and see if it was still there. That was 70 years ago and I still wonder if my name could be found on that tree trunk. Our family knew one teacher at the middle school in Yong-byon, Mr. Suk Mok Kim, who later became a professor of philosophy and ethics at the Seoul National University Teachers College. Years later, Grace and I got to know him pretty well as a highly respected professor.

Yong-byon is famous for an azalea poem written by a nationally well-known poet Kim So-Wol (Osan Middle School graduate) under the title "Azalea Flowers." Whenever I read that poem, it brings back my fond memory of the beautiful scenery of Yaksan Mountain near Yong-byon.

AZALEA FLOWERS
By Kim So-Wol

When you tire of my love
And leave me behind
Meek and silent, I shall let you go.
I shall pick an armful of azaleas
From the Yaksan hills of Yong-byon
And strew them upon your path.
You will tread softly upon the flowers,
Then step by step,
As you walk away.

When you tire of my love
And leave me behind,
Though the pain be as death
I shall not weep.

Kim So-Wol is one of the most beloved poets in Korea in spite of his early death at age 31. His verse is remarkable for the exquisite and delicate quality of its simple folk expressions. The Korean people love poems but the theme of sad separation or departure is frequent. For Korean poets, often the lover was a disguised symbol of the country Korea. Many sad love songs had to do with the loss of the country which they could not express openly while under Japanese surveillance. This poem "Azalea Flowers" is also expressive of the quiet sadness of departure with no hard feelings or bitterness, but just quiet resignation. This poem is also a good example of how Koreans tend to express and describe their feelings indirectly when one could not make direct references in politically sensitive situations.

Surrounding the mountain in Yong-byon were many mulberry trees. Silkworms eat mulberry leaves and there were many silk manufacturing factories in Yong-byon. Silk was a major industry and source of revenue for that community. While living in Yong-byon, my youngest brother Ik Poong (Paul) was born. This peaceful beautiful village of Yong-byon with the famous Yaksan Mountains nearby and full of pretty azaleas and many mulberry trees, has transformed into a world news headline because in Yong-byon the North Korean government has developed its nuclear power capacity to build a nuclear bomb. What a change from such a beautiful village to a menacing, threatening place with a nuclear bomb!!

[2-5] Transfer back to Sinuiju: After three years of working at Yong-byon, father was transferred back to the main office of the Department of Civil Engineering of P'yonganbuk-Do Province in Sinuiju, the province's capital city. After our family moved back to Sinuiju, I enrolled in Wakadake Elementary School. This school's principal was Japanese and there were more Japanese teachers there than Korean teachers. The school was operated in a more Japanese traditional manner.

Family photo in Sinuiju in 1940. Back row from right to left father, author, younger sister IK Nan, Ik Sung, and My mother holding Ik Poong.

[2-6] Change from Korean name to Japanese

name: The Japanese government was becoming more militaristic and was now urging Koreans to pledge their allegiance to the Japanese Emperor and to attend religious ceremonies at the Shinto shrine. Later the Japanese government ordered Koreans to change their Korean names to Japanese names voluntarily. The children of those Koreans who did not change their names were refused admittance to schools and Korean adults who kept their Korean names were refused public employment. The enforcement of these rules resulted in more and more "voluntary" name changes. Within six months 79% of Koreans changed their names. I had to change my name from Kim Ik-chang to a Japanese name of "Yoshikane Matsumasa." Actually, my Korean name in Chinese characters remained the same, except for adding one name in the beginning "Yoshi" which is the Japanese pronunciation anyway. When my entire name is spoken in the Japanese language, it sounds like: Yoshi-kane Matsu-masa.

At the Wakadake Elementary School, the Japanese female teachers were generally kinder and gentler than Japanese male teachers who were militaristic in attitude. The school's educational philosophy was collectivistic rather than individually oriented. For example, one student in our class was making noise talking with the student next to him. Under the Japanese educational philosophy, the entire class was responsible for correcting the malfeasant's misbehavior. The whole class was subject to punishment.

The teacher told the whole class, "Put out both of your hands with the palms up." Then he hit our outstretched palms with a bamboo stick ruler very hard, one by one. Then the teacher told the class, "The teacher and students are equally responsible for a student's misbehavior of making noise by talking with other students. I'd like to ask the class monitor to come to me and hit my hands also as a punishment." When the teacher put out his hands, the class monitor hesitated to hit the teacher's hands. Then the teacher almost shouted to the monitor, "Hit my hands with the ruler, hard and fast!" Later when the class was over, the monitor told the class that he pretended to hit their teacher's palms with the ruler, but could not hit him very hard.

When I was in elementary school, I had a close classmate friend who used to visit our home and bring his electric toys. If the electric toy didn't work, he would disassemble and repair the toy. Through this friend I became more technically oriented and interested in the subject of electricity. This made me aware that I myself had been very influenced by even my childhood friends and that this important exposure to new ideas through others may have a lifelong impact on my adult interests and behavior. My childhood friend seeded my continuing interest in the area of high technology.

[2-7] Reverend Han Kyung-Jik and his church:

In Sinuiju my parents were members of the Second Sinuiju Presbyterian Church. Reverend Han Kyung-Jik was the senior pastor and my father served as a deacon. Reverend Han graduated from Osan Middle School and P'yongyang Presbyterian Seminary. In the 1920s he went to the United States, studied at the Princeton Theological Seminary and graduated from the seminary in 1929. He later returned to Sinuiju. Reverend Han served at the Second Sinuiju Presbyterian Church for 9 years from 1933-1942. In 1939, he had organized and ran an orphanage. He understood the sufferings of the Korean people deeply and urged them to have courage and determination through faith and a devoted Christian life.

After World War II ended, Reverend Han left north Korea and went to Seoul where with twenty-seven dedicated followers he re-establish the former church named Bethany Mission School and converted a Japanese Shinto shrine into a Christian church. In November, 1946, they changed the church's name from Bethany to Youngnak Presbyterian Church (1945-1972). When our family fled to Seoul in March, 1946, we joined Youngnak Presbyterian Church where Grace and I met and continued to see each other. Youngnak Presbyterian Church was more than a church where people worshiped God. It became the place where people would meet, exchange information, get help in job seeking, and it became the model for excellent social services. Reverend Han became one of the leading Christian ministers in South Korea. He also played an important role as the principal interpreter for the Billy Graham Crusade held in Seoul for many years.

Whenever settling elsewhere as refugees and immigrants, Reverend Han's disciples and followers carried the name of "Youngnak Presbyterian Church" establishing new affiliated churches in different parts of Korea and overseas in the United States and South America. In fact, my younger son Danny and his family attend the Los Angeles Youngnak Presbyterian Church English Ministry. At that church, Danny is plays drum with church bands for the contemporary worship service. Reverend Han was the most famous and accomplished ministers in Korea. In 1992, he received the Templeton Award for his contribution.

Rev. Han Kyung Jik interpreted for Billy Graham Crusade held in
Seoul Korea in 1949.

[2-8] Cho Man Shik as the head of the temporary national government:
At the end of World War II, there was a democratic oriented national government led by Cho Man Shik prior to the takeover by the communist government of Kim IL Sung. At that time my father was appointed as Chief of the Department of Civil Engineering of P'yonganbuk-Do Province. He made many business trips to different areas of the province and supervised civil engineering projects such as water irrigation systems, tunnels, and the railroad.

Cho Man Shik, the head of provisional nationalistic democratic government
prior to Kim IL Sung's take over (1945-1946)

[2-9] Osan Middle School: After finishing elementary school, I applied for admission at Sinuiju Technical Middle School on the advice of my father, who wanted me to study engineering. I was 12 years old and World War II and the Japanese occupation of Korea was ongoing. The application process included a physical exam and at that exam the student next to me was telling a joke that made me laugh. A teacher saw me laughing and asked for my name and number. That is how we, me and the student who told the joke, were denied admission to that school. As a result, I applied for admission to the Osan Middle School which was located in Jung-Ju about two hundred miles away from my hometown of Sinuiju. In looking back it was a blessing in disguise and a good decision to attend the well-known Osan Middle School, which is equivalent to a junior high school.

Brass band members of Osan Middle School, far right standing is Luke Kim (trombone player) and the left back is Young Il Lee MD (1945 photo)

Osan Middle School alumni year end party in *2010*. LUKE I.C. Kim

My Osan Middle School experience was much more meaningful and important to my development than if I had attended that technical school for several reasons. The school was well known for its tradition of having teachers who were patriotic Korean scholars and leaders. As a private school, it emphasized the teaching of Korean history and Korean thought. The founding principal of Osan Middle School was Mr. Lee Seung Hoon. He was one of thirty-three signers of the Declaration of Independence during the March 1, 1919 Independence Movement demonstration. He was a Korean nationalist who set the tone and direction for the school. The Osan Middle School was a bastion for developing Korean patriotism and philosophy. They had excellent teachers and their graduates became well known in Korean history such as Cho Manshik (politics), Kim So-Wol (poet), Ham Sukhun (religion), Lee Kwangsoo (literature), Hwang Sunwon (literature), Kim Kyoshin (religion), Han Kyung-jik (religion), and Lim Youngryun (art).

Osan Middle School had a student housing system whereby the school assigned new freshmen with a senior to the same room. The senior assigned to me was not only inspiring to me and interested in my future career, but also enjoyed discussing the Korean national patriotic spirit. He encouraged me to write a daily diary and short essays on subjects that he assigned. He read my essays every day and corrected and improved my sentences. I remember vividly that one of the subjects he assigned to me was "firefly" so I went out to see fireflies in the rice paddy and wrote my essay. After graduation my senior roommate was admitted to Tokyo Imperial University. Unfortunately, I lost contact with him and I cannot remember his name.

I do remember my classmate Lee Ki-Moon who was the son of an apple orchard owner in Jung-ju. We used to get together once a week after we had read books of general nature which we had selected and assigned to each other. After reading these books, we met and exchanged our thoughts. Later Lee Ki-Moon became an outstanding chairman of the Department of Korean Literature at Seoul National University. His brother Lee Ki-Baek is a well-known scholar of Korean history. Looking back and comparing ourselves with contemporary junior high school students, I feel that we were much more serious about studying hard, self-improvement, and choosing future careers.

When I was at Osan Middle School, Japan was at war with the United States. We were forced to participate in military training drills as well as exercise in Judo and Kendo martial arts. Once a month, all students were assembled and mobilized into lines and marched to a nearby Shinto temple for worship. Christian churches were forced to close down all church activities. All class subjects were taught in Japanese. The Osan Middle School principal then was Japanese and education was in the Japanese style emphasizing military training and preparedness in case of an American invasion of Korean shores. There were two ROTC officers in charge of the students' military training, First Lieutenant Hayashi, and another ROTC officer whose name I have forgotten.

In spite of Japan's emphasis on military training, the nationalistic spirit of Korean independence remained strong because the majority of Osan Middle School teachers were Koreans. The spirit of Korean patriotism was generally embraced by the Osan student body. I particularly remember one Korean art teacher who had studied fine arts at Yale University in the United States and was active in the artist circles of Paris. This art teacher, Youngryun Lim, taught us not only fine arts but also conversational English which was quite different from other middle schools in Korea where English classes focused mainly on grammar and sentence structure without lessons in conversational English. My art teacher motivated me to pursue and continue to develop my conversational English skills.

[2-10] Japan's general mobilization order for Korean students to hard labor: My entire ninth grade class at Osan Middle School, about 150 of us, was rounded up, taken away as a group from the school, and forced to work and live in a military ammunitions factory complex in P'yongyang. P'yongyang was the largest city in the northern part of Korea and is now the capital of North Korea. The ammunitions factory was located about 100 miles from our school. I was 14 years old at the time. The factory complex in P'yongyang occupied a huge area with rows of factory buildings where all kinds of bombs, bullets, and canon shells were produced. The compound was completely surrounded by high brick walls with barbed wire on the top and was guarded by Japanese soldiers. In "our" weapons factory, there must have been at least a thousand "mobilized" middle school students, 14 and 15 year old boys, coming from different middle schools. The factory ran 24 hours continuously and we worked in three shifts under the close watch of Japanese soldiers. In those days, the middle schools were not co-educational; there were separate schools for boys and girls.

Our Osan Middle School students were housed together in a large open warehouse type building that had a wooden floor. We were each issued a thin mattress and a blanket to sleep with on the wooden floor. Every morning when we got up, we folded our mattresses and blankets and piled them neatly against the wall. We all wore work uniforms. We lived completely as a group under strict militaristic rules and discipline. A Japanese Imperial Army platoon was attached to our work unit to supervise and control our movements and activities. Three times a day, we stood in formation and marched briskly in a military style to and from our living quarters and the mess hall. The three daily meals were the same: a bowl of barley rice, a cup of thin soup with a condiment of bean sprouts and once in a while a few pieces of seasoned turnip (*taku-ang*) or apricot pickled with vinegar and red coloring (*umeboshi*.) We were always hungry. There was very little individual free time. When we were not working in the factory, we slept and ate together or conducted military drills and exercises. We were given a brief basic training in how to operate the lathe machine. My assigned task was to use the lathe to trim the cast iron outer shell of a bomb casing to an exact size and shape. Other students made different ammunition shells. The factory had poor air circulation, was rather dark, and was filled with machine noise. Often I was assigned to work the night shift, and slept for six to eight hours during the day. During the one year and six months while we were interned there, we had one opportunity to go outside of the factory compound and barbed wire walls and that was for participating in a military exercise. It was a prison life with forced labor. Over time we learned that the girls were mobilized and interned to work in garment factories making military uniforms as well as clothes for soldiers using sewing machines. One of the tenth grade classmates (one year senior to our class), Mr. Yunduk Kim, told us that his entire tenth grade classmates were sent to a fertilizer factory near the Yalu River to do hard labor work there, and that they were also forced to do hard labor carrying stones and soil to build up the banks of the Yalu River near the Sinuiju airport.

[2-11] News at the weapons factory of the end of WWII on August 15, 1945: On the morning of August 15, 1945, we were all ordered to assemble in the big open playground to hear Japanese Emperor Hirohito announcing the end of World War II by unconditional surrender to the allied forces. There were at least about 2000 students present. At that gathering I saw for the first time female high school students as well as students from other middle schools. At first we did not know what Emperor Hirohito was saying because he spoke in

a peculiar royal-style of Japanese. Later on when we finally understood that Japan had surrendered and that the Japanese occupation would end, we were surprised because the Japanese mass media and propaganda had convinced us throughout the war that Japan was winning. We did not know anything about the dropping of atomic bombs on Hiroshima and Nagasaki. The Japanese newspapers did briefly and vaguely make reference to a new type of bomb being developed and dropped by the U.S. Air Force. From where we were in Korea, we could sense that not everything was going right in the war. We saw B-29s flying over us several times, and we were secretly glad and happy to see them.

After the announcement ending World War II, we were allowed to go outside the factory gates into P'yongyang city where people on the street were shouting with joy *"mansei"* (long life) for Korean Independence. Instead of walking individually, we marched together on the P'yongyang streets. Unfortunately, the end of World War II came with the political tragedy of dividing Korea into two political entities.

[2-12] Return to Osan Middle School: After the war was over, we were finally freed from the forced hard labor work for one and a half year at P'yongyang weapons factory. We packed and returned to Osan Middle School in Jung-Ju town by train. When we returned the school was in a state of confusion and transition and not quite ready to resume classes.

We learned later from a group of our senior Osan students who went to the Japanese ROTC officer, Lieutenant Hayashi's home, and found out a pistol lying near his body. Apparently, out of shame and anger over the Japanese defeat, Lieutenant Hayashi shot his pregnant wife and then shot himself with his pistol. They further said that Lieutenant Hayashi must have felt very disappointed and enraged with feelings of shame and resentment over the Japanese Emperor's surrender.

At the urging of senior classmates, they decided to cremate him before the funeral. Because I was a class president, I was asked to pick up his bones with chopsticks and place them in the urn. I did perform the task out of duty, but I experienced profoundly eerie, strange and mixed feelings because, on one hand, I was glad that the Japanese army was defeated, but on the other hand I felt humanitarian, sorry feelings over the demise of Lieutenant Hayashi and his pregnant wife. The other ROTC officer also became demoralized to the point where he looked quite different with a runny nose, shaggy hair, dirty clothes, and stooped posture in the way he walked. I was so surprised to see how quickly a person can change from being arrogant and proud to being demoralized and very sad in appearance and behavior. I came to realize how important morale can influence human behavior.

After my return to the Osan Middle School, I rejoined the school band and played the trombone. I recall when General Yonggun Choi of the North Korean Army, an Osan graduate, visited our school. He had traveled to China where he joined the Chinese Communist Army, became a communist, and now came back to North Korea after its liberation. General Choi was a student and follower of Cho Manshik who was teaching at Osan Middle School. His visit to Osan seemed to have purpose of urging the students not to participate in anti-communism and anti-Russia demonstrations. Our school band played welcoming and marching music during General Choi's inspection of the student parade.

[2-13] My first encounter with Soviet (Russian) soldiers: After the war, I realized Russian soldiers were occupying the northern part of Korea and influencing the security conditions by assisting the North Korean forces. The Russian officers were generally white Caucasian Russians and the enlisted soldiers were multi-racial, appearing to have come from Central Asia, the Middle East, and Asia. After the end of World War II and the liberation of Korea, I transferred from Osan Middle School to Dong-Joong Middle School in order to be with my family in Sinuiju. On my train trip home from Jung-Ju, I encountered Russian soldiers in the railroad station who checked my belongings and took my aluminum lunchbox. At the train station, I observed that Russians liked roasted sunflower seeds because there were many sunflower seed shells left on the platform where the Russian soldiers stood.

I remember vividly a street scene in Sinuiju at the end of World War II when the first group of Soviet Army soldiers entered my hometown. They looked disheveled, dirty, primitive, uneducated, and many acted like immature and silly adolescents. They behaved as if they had never experienced civilized living. The soldiers would stop Korean people on the street and take their watches, gold rings, and any other items that looked interesting or curious to them. They were giggling and shouting with excitement as they were touching and stealing from Korean people. Some soldiers would wear a dozen or more watches on the same arm and then show them off to their fellow soldiers.

Then Russian soldiers began to invade Korean houses during the night and demanded women, shouting "Madam! Madam!" About two or three soldiers did come to our house once. They looked around every corner of the house to see if there were any women. My mother hid inside a cabinet and luckily avoided their detection. Because Koreans did not know the Russian language, and vice versa, communication with the Russian soldiers was difficult. Our neighbors in Sinuiju developed a warning system for sending signals to their neighbors whenever Russian soldiers were in the neighborhood. The person in the first house would strike empty cans with a stick like playing a drum to make a loud noise, and then the next neighbor would likewise transmit the signal to the next neighbor in a relay fashion thus warning all neighbors that the Russians were coming. Sometimes, especially this signaling system had the effect of chasing the Russian soldiers away from the neighborhood.

During this period of growing Russian presence in the north, the Osan Middle School played a peculiar humanitarian role by gathering and putting Japanese people in a dormitory to protect the Japanese women from sexual violence by the Russian soldiers.

[2-14] Kim IL Sung as head of communist North Korea: After liberation and prior to the establishment of a communist government by Kim IL Sung, there was a democratically oriented nationalistic provisional government under the leadership of Cho Manshik. He appointed my father to be the director of the Department of Civil Engineering in P'yonganbuk-Do Province. My father had high respect for Cho Manshik and his political stands. My father had to go away from home often in order to fulfill his responsibilities as the Director of Civil Engineering, including going to P'yongyang to see Cho Manshik.

The occupying Soviet military forces helped the Korean communists organize and establish the Communist Party and the North Korean communist military and police organizations. Eventually they installed the North Korean communist government headed by Kim IL Sung. Kim IL Sung was reportedly a Korean who had been a military officer in the Soviet army. The Soviets armed the North Korean communists with weapons they confiscated from the Japanese army. This was in violation of the superpower agreement that each occupying force was to destroy the weapons confiscated from Japanese soldiers in disarmament. The American forces occupying South Korea burned or dumped confiscated Japanese weapons into the ocean.

In 1946, the United Nations proposed that a general election be held in both North and South Korea under the supervision of the United Nations. North Korea rejected the proposal and on their own established Kim IL Sung as their president without a free democratic general election. A general election was held in South Korea under the supervision of the United Nations, and Syngman Rhee was elected as the first president of the Republic of Korea (South Korea). Syngman Rhee was one of the Korean Independence fighters and leaders who organized support for the Korean Independence movement in the United States.

When we returned to Sinuiju, my parents acquired and moved the family into a Japanese style house. In that neighborhood, I observed that there were many young Japanese women living with high-ranking Russian soldiers. I later heard that these Japanese women had a mission of protecting the interests and security of other Japanese residents by providing "(sexual) comfort" to Russian soldiers prior to the Japanese residents being returned to Japan. These young Japanese women living with Russian soldiers remind me of the many young Korean women who had to be involved with American military personnel in order to make money to support their parents and siblings. Later on many of these Korean women married the soldiers, migrated to the United States, and brought their parents and siblings to the United States as immigrants. We need to appreciate these Korean women whose sacrifice and devotion to their families' survival were instrumental in the growth of the Korean American population in the United States.

[2-15] The Sinuiju student uprising incident:

As I previously mentioned, I transferred from Osan Middle School to Dong-Joong ("East") Middle School in Sinuiju in order to join my family residing there. Following the end of World War II and the Korean liberation from Japanese occupation, the communist government began to establish North Korea as an independent political entity. The middle school teachers in Sinuiju were completely reshuffled and the school curriculum drastically changed, especially the history class. The curriculum was changed to study the history of communism and the Bolshevik movement in Russia. The Korean literature class was changed to primarily study the poems and novels of communist writers.

My 8th and 9th grade classmates in Dong-Joong Middle School became very unhappy, infuriated and rebellious over the reassignment of teachers and curriculum changes. After their negotiations with school authorities about the curriculum changes failed, the students decided to demonstrate with a protest march on the street near the school. The students were unhappy and their complaints became louder and louder up to the boiling point.

On November 16, 1945, an Assembly of the Social Democratic Party of Yonganpo in P'yonganbuk-Do Province was held. At the Assembly meeting, the Dong-Joong students demonstrated, demanding that the Russian military army withdraw from Korea and protesting the school curriculum changes towards communist ideology. In support of the student demands, about five thousand students from six Sinuiju middle schools gathered on November 23, 1945, and began to demonstrate in the street, shouting "Academic freedom!" In response to the increasing intensity of the student demonstration, the communist government security forces with the support of Russian soldiers, including airplanes, moved to quash the demonstration.

I was then a third year student (9th grader in U.S. system) at Dong-Joong Middle School. I joined the student demonstration on the street shouting for academic freedom. I saw three Russian-made reconnaissance airplanes circle and spray machinegun bullets at us while we were demonstrating in the street. Some of the machine gun bullets hit the ground, making smoking traces of dust in the air. One of the students with me was shot. The students scattered in different directions seeking hiding places, including myself. From there, I went home. According to the older brother of a friend of mine, some students ran to his home to hide from the Russian soldiers who were coming after them. The Russian soldiers had come later to his home and arrested students who were hiding there.

According to Osan alumnus Mr. Yunduk Kim, Osan Middle School students went to the Jung-Ju train station intending to travel and join the ongoing Sinuiju student protests. After hearing about the Russian-made airplanes shooting at the Sinuiju demonstrators, Osan teachers discouraged their students from going and the students responded by not joining the protest.

The communist government's effort to curtail the demonstrations resulted in twenty students being killed and seven hundred injured. About two thousand were arrested and put into jail. This incident was historically significant and an important event in Korean history because the Sinuiju Students Demonstration Against Communism was Korea's first student-led protest against communism and the Soviet Union occupation. This demonstration however is almost unknown to the outside world.

[2-16] Modern Exodus from North Korea: The

North Korean communist government began to purge leaders in political, academic, religious fields and civic organizations who were not members of the Communist Party. Many Christian ministers and Christian believers were targeted. Many North Korean citizens could not tolerate and cope with the total control over their lives imposed by the authoritarian Stalinist-style communist government. They fled from North Korea to escape the large-scale purging and oppression. Thousands and thousands of Koreans crossed the 38th parallel to find new lives in South Korea. By the end of 1947, the number of those who fled North Korea rose sharply, totaling more than 800,000. Eventually more than 3 million Koreans crossed the dangerous 38th parallel border (Lee, KB, 1984). Some people called the massive escape from North Korea the first "modern exodus" of the post-World War II era.

The exodus from North Korea caused numerous tragic human stories. Many family members were separated because the departures had to be sudden and secretive, leaving some family members behind permanently. To this date, thousands of separated family members have never been able to contact or reunite with each other, including my relatives. These family separations occurred more than sixty years ago.

My uncle was a Presbyterian minister who was ordained by American Presbyterian missionaries. He was kidnapped and imprisoned because he was a highly respected church leader. We heard later that he was sent to a hard labor camp near Siberia. I still have many aunts, nephews, cousins and other relatives living in North Korea, but since 1946 I have not been able to establish contact with any of them.

In the past, the South Korean Government has made several proposals to North Korean government to establish an exchange program of family visitation between North and South Koreas. The North Korean government tends to playing on and off games, by responding to geopolitical and internal national dynamics.

[2-17] Father's escape from North Korea to South

Korea by fishing boat: My father was a university-educated civil

engineer. For most of his life, he designed and supervised the construction of highways, dams, tunnels and water irrigation systems in the northern part of Korea. After Korea was liberated from Japanese occupation, my father became the director of the Department of Civil Engineering Department of P'yonganbuk-Do Province in the provisional government led by Cho Manshik.

As time went on, the power of the Communist Party increased and they began to purge Christian leaders. Then the Communists arrested Cho Manshik and those who supported his policies and his democratically oriented nationalistic provisional government. They were all arrested on bogus charges.

My father was tipped off by a good friend who belonged to the Communist Party. The friend came to our home and told father, "Everybody knows that you belong to Cho Manshik's government. They are going to arrest you on a bogus charge. Therefore, I urge you to flee from Sinuiju." My father had to leave town suddenly and secretly. He headed to South Korea on a fishing boat. About two months later, the rest of family also escaped to avoid arrest and detention by the communist government.

[2-18] My father's diary on his escape by sea:
"On the way, the ship encountered heavy rain and a strong wind. The ship was unable to sail forward. Therefore it was anchored near the seashore. Even during the anchoring on the shore, the wind was so strong that the rope attached to the anchor almost broke and they were afraid that the ship might drift off into the ocean and be destroyed. If the rain and wind had continued another ten or fifteen minutes, the rope would have been completely cut off and the ship would have drifted to the ocean. However, fortunately, the rain and strong wind stopped. Two or three days later, the ship arrived at the Cho-Do village and was searched by local security. I was hiding at the bottom of the ship. I heard the footsteps. However, the ship's captain bribed the security forces which allowed the ship to leave the seashore without being sent to Jin-Nam-Po. It took ten days for the ship to arrive at the Mapo Harbor in South Korea and that was April 7, 1946."

[2-19] The rest of the family escaping south through the 38th Parallel:
About two months after my father left to go south, the rest of my family decided to escape from North Korea through the 38th Parallel. In June, 1946, my mother, my younger sister Ik Nan, and two younger brothers Ik Sung and Ik Poong, and I (16 years old) quietly left Sinuiju at dawn. We wore ragged clothes and smeared charcoal ashes on our faces to disguise ourselves as refugees returning to Korea from

China. Only those Korean refugees from China were allowed to move from one city to another. My mother instructed us several times that whenever people asked us, we should say, "We are Korean refugees from China going back to Korea."

We secretly acquired train tickets from somebody who was connected with the train station and got on a train at the Sinuiju train station without difficulty. While we were passing through Jung-Ju on the train, we saw the Osan Middle School building for the last time. I felt my heart beat faster while I was thinking of my days at Osan Middle School and the future of the school. When we arrived at Sariwon, the train station furthest south, we were told we would have to walk from there to the 38th Parallel. Before our departure from Sariwon, mother hired a local guide for lots of money and he led us for the next ten days or so. While waiting for an appropriate opportunity to start the trip, the guide invited us to stay at his home for a week or so. This local guide and the North Korean security guard nearby seemed to know each other and discussed the best time for us to go through the 38th Parallel checkpoint.

One early morning, after a several days stay at the guide's home, he said, "Let's go now. Today is the day to cross the 38th Parallel." So we loaded our belongings supposedly carried from China on top of a wagon pulled by an ox. When we arrived at the North Korean security station, one of the security men came out and told my mother that he needed to inspect the boxes on the oxcart. He added, "If I open the belongings, I'll probably discover lots of jewelry and treasures." Then my mother told the security person, "We are Korean refugees from China returning to my home in South Korea." At about the same moment, there was a loud voice coming from inside the security office shouting, "They are refugees from China going back to Korea. So, we don't have to open their belongings. Let them pass through!" After this shouting announcement, the security guard stopped and allowed us to pass through without any inspection of our boxes and belongings. The second security guard who had shouted the announcement from inside came out and told us, "You can go now. Just follow the road toward the south. Then you will be okay." He appeared to be the boss of the security guard who tried to open our belongings.

Those who tried to cross the 38th Parallel going south included two kinds of people: those Korean refugees who actually lived in China and were returning to South Korea, and those North Korean residents who hated the communist government and were trying to escape to South

Korea. The security guards treated these two groups quite differently. They treated the North Koreans escaping from the North very harshly. They permitted free or easy passage across the border checkpoint to the Korean refugees actually returning from China. North Koreans who tried to cross the 38th Parallel border during the night were often shot. If caught by the military guards, they were arrested and sent to prison. A considerable number of North Koreans trying to escape oppression in the north died in this manner. We learned that hundreds and thousands of North Koreans were shot and arrested at the 38th Parallel during their escape attempts.

As indicated above, it was due to our luck and risky but brave act that we were able to cross the 38th parallel through the security station without any difficulty. We started walking carrying our belongings on our shoulders. After a while, we saw several South Korean people waiting to greet us. These South Koreans assisted those like our family just arriving from the north by offering a helping hand and carrying our belongings.

After we made our successful escape to South Korea, we cried with joy, kneeled down for prayer, and kissed the soil. We thanked God, and vowed our dedication to God's work. Freedom of religion was important to us, and it was one of the important reasons why we had to leave North Korea.

The greeters took us and our belongings by truck to the refugee camp in Kae-Sung (which has now become part of North Korea whereas it was part of the South Korea prior to the Korean War). As soon as we arrived at the refugee camp, U.S. soldiers came and sprayed our entire bodies with DDT insecticide. Then they gave us food and a place to sleep for a couple of nights. My first interesting sight was the American soldiers. They were clean cut, well dressed, friendly and smiling which was quite a contrast to the Russian soldiers who stole watches and sought out women. The American soldiers handed out candies and chocolates to the children.

After staying two nights at the refugee camp, we went to Seoul by train and met our maternal uncle Choo Dae Byuk who owned a Japanese style two story house in the Seodae Moon (West Gate) district in Seoul. There we found our father who had been living there for a while. We were all so glad to be reunited with our father.I was fifteen years old at that time.

[2-20] Our life in Seoul prior to the Korean War:

We worked hard to establish our lives in Seoul, the capital of South Korea. We lived in uncle Choo Dae Byuk's house. Our family of six—my parents and four children—occupied a 10 X 12 feet room with a veranda. We slept, ate, played, and studied in that "multi-purpose" room while our mother cooked meals on a Coleman stove on the veranda.

The room next to our room on the second floor was occupied by my cousin, Choo Bong-noong, who was a student at Severance Medical School. He was picked up and drafted into the North Korean Army as a medical doctor and was later killed in battle. My cousin Choo Li shared that room and later she became a famous Spanish Flamenco dancer and the only Korean in the Spanish Royal Ballet Dance Group in Spain. After returning to Korea, she has been running a Spanish Ballet Studio in Seoul. My orphaned cousins Ae Nah, Bong Duk and Neung Duk lived with our grandmother downstairs.

My father got a job as a civil engineer in a construction company. We stayed at uncle's house for one year and a half until our parents saved enough to move out to our own rented house. We, the children, were enrolled in different schools. I entered Seoul High School. My sister Ik Nan entered Sookmyung Girls High School, our mother's alma mater. The principal at that time was Mrs. Moon Nam Shik, mother's classmate. Ik Nan entered the school without any difficulty. My brothers Ik Sung and Ik Poong went to the Duksoo Elementary School. I was too young to realize, but later learned to appreciate my mother's continuing efforts to place us in the best schools available in Korea. During this period, we had a relatively peaceful and happy life even though we were poor.

[2-21] Family activities: When I was in high school and living in the Seodai Moon (West Gate) district, we attended a small Methodist Church and were members of their youth group. Our most memorable Christmas and Easter Sunday were at this church. That Easter Sunday we were a part of the youth AMEN group and sang early sunrise Easter hymns in front of different church members' homes. We also went caroling at Christmas. I carried the flute and played the first several measures of songs as a prelude and then the chorus would join in song. I will never forget how happy, pure and uplifted I was in those days despite the difficult conditions.

On Easter Sunday, the minister wanted a big poster picture for the wall behind the pulpit depicting the resurrected Christ ascending into a cloud. There was no large poster paper available, so I pasted together small size paper with glue to make a large sheet. My sister Ik Nan drew a picture of Christ ascending into a cloud with light shining over his head. Everybody admired the picture and asked who drew it. They were told that it was done by one of the AMEN group members. Ik Nan was very pleased with her work and said how happy and blessed she would be if she could devote and contribute her life to the work and mission of the church through the medium of fine arts.

In that year Ik Nan also drew another poster picture for Christmas. It was Mary holding a baby with Joseph looking on. That picture came out well and was posted behind the pulpit and everybody liked it. We did a sacred Christmas drama in which Ik Nan played the role of Mary. In those days we were totally immersed in church life and it was one of the happiest times in our lives.

One summer at church there was a speech contest that IkNan participated in. The title was: "Breakdown the Wall of the 38th Parallel!" She drafted the speech and consulted with uncle Choo Dae Byuk (Choo Li's father), who was a great orator. My sister and I went to the empty church building, where she practiced her speech. I listened and gave her feedback. When she shouted, "Don't you agree with me?" in her speech with her fist pounding on the table, I urged her, "Louder! Louder!" At the end of the practice, I applauded and said, "That's good. Do it like that." She won second place in that contest. The first place was won by a male student, who later became chairman of the Department of Chemistry at Yonsei University, Dr. Seung Moo Lee. The following year, Ik Nan took part in another speech contest. The title was something like, "Is Religion Opium or Real Religion?" My sister and I prepared for the contest again, and I think she won one of the prizes. Those were memorable and happy days for us.

People say that I'm always helping others behind the scene, just as I helped my sister with her speech contests. I have always been very close to Ik Nan and helped and advised her on projects at church. Grace also said that I am supportive of what she does, and I like my behind-the-scene supportive role.

[2-22] My experiences at Seoul High School: By passing English and math examinations I was admitted into the fifth grade of Seoul High School (equivalent to 11th grade in the American system.) In those old days, Korean elementary school was six years of study followed by middle/high school was an additional six year curriculum. The Korean middle and high school is equivalent to the combined junior and senior high schools of the American system. In the American system, 1st grade to 12th grade is counted from elementary school through high school continuously. In the Korean system, the counting starts all over again with middle school having a 1st year class through 6th year class. The current

Korean educational system has adopted the American system of junior high and senior high school, and did away with middle school.

Seoul High School was originally called the Kyung Sung Middle School during the Japanese occupation. After Korean Independence, the name changed to Seoul High School. Under the leadership of Principal Kim Won Kyu, the school had many excellent teachers and students from the north who escaped to South Korea. The principal, who had a strong charisma, was very strict with his students. During this period there were some intense street demonstrations in Seoul led by leftist students. Principal Kim prevented his students from participating in these demonstrations with strict discipline and supervision. He would suspend students who were absent from school and forced them to study late at school. The school had a reputation as a first-class school with 90% of its graduates going on to university. I cannot forget the morning assemblies on school yard where Principal Kim spoke over the microphone, almost preached, to the entire student body for more than an hour every morning from Monday to Friday. Through his long inspiring speeches, he always emphasized the historical mission and responsibility that we each had and that "We must become an indispensable and essential person." Every school day began with Principal Kim's long and stirring speeches of encouragement.

During his travels to England, Principal Kim visited and inspected various schools. He found out that British students were to take a nap for 30 to 40 minutes after lunch and that practice improved their study effectiveness. He decided to implement a similar system at Seoul High School. After lunch students were forced to take a nap for 30 minutes either in the classroom or on the lawn. Holding a short stick in his hand, he checked to see whether his students were sleeping or not. Some students who found it difficult to sleep or did not feel like sleeping pretended to sleep when the principal approached. Seoul High School students were not used to sleeping during the day and found it difficult to adapt to such a system. Principal Kim abolished the system shortly after it had been initiated.

Principal Kim did not like young students who kept their hands in their pockets because to him the practice appeared ugly, careless and looked arrogant or lazy. He ordered students to sew up their trouser pockets so that they did not have any pockets at all. He required school uniforms because it was very important to him that his students had clean cut appearances. For an extracurricular activity, I joined the Seoul High School Chorus. The Seoul High School Chorus had won the high school choral contest three times in a row and we were often invited to sing for VIP international guests visiting Korea. I remember U.N. Secretary General Vengalil Menon applauding us for our rendition of "Blue Danube" at his reception.

Whenever I think about Seoul High school, I cannot forget about a fellow classmate of mine, Ik Hyun Kong. In fact, he and I shared the same desk in the class rooms, and studied together as one of my closest friends. He is somewhat an odd-ball, but genius in math and science. In the advance algebra class, for example, he would make an embarrassing question to the math teacher, pointing out the easier way of solving the problems than the teacher approached, and/or pointing out the mistake the teacher made in solving a math problem on the black board.

When we advanced to a graduating class, all of us were preparing for college entrance examinations. However, I noticed that Ik Hyun was studying the Russian language and that he does not appear to be concerned with college entrance exam at all.

As graduation day is approaching soon, he confided to me that he was studying Russian because he hopes to go to Soviet Union in order to study the Sputnik space technology and become a aeronautic space scientist/professor. Knowing his inborn High IQ and his scientific ability and talent, I thought to myself that he is likely to become a famous scientist/ professor.

Soon after graduation from Seoul High School, one very late night, Ik Hyun showed up at our house, knocking the door. When I answered the door, Ik Hyun was there looking haggard and nervous. He said: "let me stay here overnight in your place. I am very tired now. In the morning, I will tell you everything what happened to me." While disrobing, I saw the swollen, red colored streaks of the skin on the back.

Next morning he told me the following: He was invited to a social party held at Russian Embassy in Seoul where he was able to use his Russian language so well that he impressed the Russian Ambassador and his staff. He said that the Russian Ambassador was so impressed that the Russian ambassador himself wrote a recommendation letter each to North Korean government and the Soviet Union government, recommending him as a foreign student acceptable to any prestigious universities of his choice in the Soviet Union. He hid the 2 letters inside his shoe heels, and tried to cross the 38th parallel to North Korea. He said that on his way crossing the demilitarized zone, he was detected and picked up by South Korean security guards. He was interrogated as a possible communist spy. He was whipped on his back. He had to give his identity as a recent graduate of Seoul High School, and as his reference, he gave them my name and Seoul Hi Principal, Mr. Won Kyu Kim. After checking with Principal Mr. Kim, they released him free.

After graduation from Seoul High School, I was accepted to, and entered, Seoul National University, College of Liberal Arts and Science as a premedical student.

In the meantime, I was very busy schooling, and did not think much about my friend, lk Hyun, nor heard about him at all for quite a while.

One year passed after my high school graduation, and when I became a 2nd year premed student, the Korean War broke out, on June25, 1950. And then everything went hay wired.

In the meantime, I wondered whether my friend lk Hyun was able to go to the Soviet Union according to his plan, until I met another Seoul Hi classmate, Seung Moo lee who had the answer. We had several oddball genius including Mr. Lee who were ahead of time. Mr. Seung Moo Lee was very good at chemistry and biochemistry when we were in Seoul Hi School. Eventually he became professor and chairman of the department of chemistry and organic chemistry at Yonsei University, Seoul Korea.

Mr. Lee told me the following events and story about lk Hyun.

Mr. Lee said that during the Korean War, he was drafted to the South Korean Army. While advancing to north toward Yalu River bordering with China, his battalion was ambushed by the Chinese "Volunteer Army" and he was made a prisoner of war (POW). He said that he had rough time indeed while in the North Korean prison for POWs. For example, he told me how horrible and cruel it was to give out blankets only to 2/3 of UN-POWS, and no blanket at all to the rest of 1/3 of UN-POWs in the famous sub-zero freezing cold winter weather in North Korea prisons for UN-POWs. Every night there were big fights among the fellow POWs to grab and secure a piece of blanket. They say that the North Korean Prison Authority does this on tactical reasons for breaking up mutually cohesive and cooperative grouping among UN-POWs.

One day, to his surprise, he saw Mr. lk Hyun Kong at the prison site recognizing who he was right away as they were a long—time friend. He noticed that Mr. lk Hyun Kong wore a North Korean Army officer's uniform with a rank of Lieutenant.

Later he learned that Lt. lk Hyun Kong was assigned to this prison on a short trip with the purpose of supervising the process of deciding the choice the UN—POWs must make, that is, selecting whether they want to go back to their own country after release from POW status, or they prefer remaining in North Korea, and even given the choice of choosing a neutral 3rd country, such as India. This procedure was established because many North Korean POWs refused to be released back to North Korea, instead they prefer to remain in South Korea after released free from POW status.

While Mr. Lee was going through the procedure of choosing to return to South Korea, Lt. Kong was involved in the process as their supervisor .There Mr. Lee and Lt. Kong met each other officially for the first time. However, Lt Kong pretended not to know him and proceeded to treat Mr. Lee in a formal and routine method. Mr. Lee and Mr. Kong originally came from the same hometown, Haeju, North Korea, and transferred to Seoul High School about the same time and were in the same class. Therefore, they knew each other very well.

They know each other so well that it is impossible not to know who they were to each other.

At any rate, they did not have the opportunity to talk with each other privately.

Now at least, we know that during the Korean War, he did not go to Soviet Union to study Sputnik aerospace technology, but ended up as a North Korean Army officer.

This event happened 60 years ago, it is possible that since then, Mr. Kong may have been to Russia, or has resided in Russia even now.

It is possible also for Lt. Kong to have visited our home in Seoul to look for me (after I left for Buyo) while he was in Seoul during the Communists' occupation of Seoul, similar to my wife Grace's situation where former high school classmates who now became North Korean Army actually came to her house in Seoul to look for her (she already vacated from home, hiding in a remote country side). Actually there were many situations where the old friends now became the worst enemy by drafting forcefully their friends to the North Korean military forces.

I was also a member of the Seodae Moon Methodist Church high school youth choir where I met Chang Soo Chul, a prominent choir conductor. Through Mr. Chang, I got to know and become a close friend of Dr. Park Chai Hoon, a highly productive, highly respected sacred music composer, Lee Dong Hoon, the violinist-director of the Pilgreen Choral Society, and other well-known Korean religious musicians.

In 1949, I graduated from Seoul High School in its first graduating class as "Seoul High School" and entered Seoul National University as a premed student. There I joined the Medical School Choral Society where I met many talented vocalists, particularly excellent tenors, among the medical students. We performed the Italian opera, "Cavalleria Rusticana" at the Myung-Dong Public Hall.

After four years of living in Seoul, we had settled down quite a bit into our "refugee life." As my mother had planned, my younger brother Ik Sung completed Duksoo Elementary School and in 1947 entered Seoul High School. My sister Ik Nan graduated from Sookmyung Girls High School and in 1950 was accepted for admission to Ewha Women University with a major in fine arts. My youngest brother Ik Poong entered Seoul High School during our refugee life at Busan in 1952, and continued at Seoul High School when it moved back from its temporary site in Busan to the original school facility The schools we attended were some of the best in Korea. Father's job and income improved. After we moved to our own house, for a change our life situation improved quite a bit. It was a most peaceful and the happiest time for our family; this was the period just before the outbreak of the Korean War.

Luke Kim (marked X) in Seoul High School graduation photo

Principal of Seoul High School, Won Kyu Kim

One of the principal's teachings was "Be clean" Therefore, teachers inspected
students' cleanness during the morning assembly

Seoul High School School Band where I was a member playing trombone

Medal given to me as one of the Korean War Veterans among Seoul High School graduates. The right side medal has my name engraved.

Group picture of Korean War veterans of members of the Seoul High School alumni association in Seoul in October 2010. Luke Kim has cross on his head.

Chapter 3

Korean War (1950-1953)

[3-1] Pre-Korean War geopolitical situation of Korea:
With the prospect of victory by the Allied forces in World War II being near, the leaders of the United States, Great Britain and China met in Cairo in June, 1943, and adopted the so-called Cairo Declaration on December I, 1943, proclaiming: "The aforesaid three great powers, mindful of enslavement of the people of Korea, are determined that in due course Korea shall become free and independent" The leaders of the same three Allied nations met again in the Berlin suburb of Potsdam in July, 1945, to reaffirm the Cairo principles.

On August 15, 1945, World War II ended with the unconditional surrender of Japan, and Korea was finally liberated after 36 years of Japanese colonial occupation. The Korean people were very exuberant about the real prospect of establishing a free, independent and democratic country as one nation. However, the excitement of liberation did not last long and did not bring independence, because the ideological conflict from the Cold War between the United States and the Soviet Union resulted in a partitioned nation of Korea. Without any input from the Korean people, Korea was unfortunately divided into North Korea and South Korea arbitrarily at the 38th parallel at the convenience of the two Super Powers. Subsequently, with Soviet backing, North Korea became a Stalinist-style communist country ruled by Kim IL Sung, and then his son, Kim Jong II, and recently now grandson Kim Jung Un. In contrast, South Korea put down roots as a democratic, free market-oriented nation, becoming one of the most technologically-oriented, rapidly-industrializing nations in the world.

[3-2] Invasion of South Korea by the North Korean People's Army:

I still vividly remember the morning of June 25, 1950. That day happened to be a Sunday. In those days, I was eager to learn conversational English and I had just met an American missionary who was interested in giving me private lessons on the Bible. I accepted his offer primarily because I wanted the opportunity to improve my conversational English. After we finished our lesson, we went outside and saw two airplanes swirling around above us. I saw the red star marks on the wings definitely signifying the North Korean Air Force. We were puzzled and wondered what was going on. South Korea was totally unprepared for an all-out North Korean military invasion. The invasion was so swift that Seoul fell to the hands of the invaders in three days with little resistance.

According to one historical document (Lee, K.B. 1984), the North Korean military power consisted of as many as ten well trained infantry divisions, 242 tanks and 211 planes, all supplied by the Soviet Union. In contrast, the South Korean army had no more than eight divisions, mostly armed with rifles and some machine guns, and not a single tank and the South Korean Air Force had 20 training aircraft, but not one fighter plane.

Note: By the way, Prof. K.B. Lee is a famous historian in South Korea who graduated from Osan Middle School three years my senior.

North Korean tanks rolling on main street in Seoul

The North Korean government insisted all along, and the majority of North Korean citizens still believe, that the Korean War was started by the South Korean Army. More recent documents available from the Russian government after the demise of the old Soviet Union indicated that there was a secret meeting between Stalin and Kim IL Sung where Stalin approved Kim IL Sung's request for military assistance to conquer South Korea. They planned an all-out invasion of South Korea by the North Korean army as part of the Soviet Union's "post-World War" strategy to expand their power and influence in Asia and the world. After the North Korean forces invaded South Korea, President Truman and the United Nations (U.N.) quickly resolved to give military support to South Korea. An U.N. command was established and troops from 16 United Nations member countries arrived in Korea and fought side by side with the South Korean Army under the United Nations flag.

In three days, Seoul was completely encircled and trapped by the North Korean army. Very few were able to escape from Seoul and all the remaining Seoul citizens became captives of the North Korean Army. Rows of North Korean tanks rolled along the streets of Seoul. We heard the explosive sounds of cannons as well as of anti-aircraft guns. I peeked into the main street from an alley and saw North Korean foot soldiers marching in formation, singing and shouting in high spirits celebrating the conquest of Seoul. Big placards and post-sign slogans were hung all over the streets, praising and saluting the life-size portrait of Kim IL Sung. Street signs were also posted urging Seoul citizens to surrender themselves to "the bosom of the fatherland." The signs promised food and protection if the citizens of Seoul would come out from hiding. Seoul residents depended on the daily delivery of food supplies from rural regions. In order to choke off the food supply heading to Seoul, the North Korean Army blocked all the roads and stopped all the traffic. All transportation routes into Seoul were cut off by the North Korean Army. Seoul's food supplies became depleted with no prospect of new supplies. The citizenry knew that they could not survive with the food they had on hand. The communists' strategy was that sooner or later people would come out of hiding and surrender if they starved long enough.

Seoul railroad station completely destroyed

[3-3] My "hiding place" and the kidnapping of my mother:

When the Korean War broke out, my father was in a southern part of South Korea supervising an agricultural irrigation system construction project. Because he was away from Seoul, he was the only person in our family who was able to avoid the communist occupation of Seoul. All the grain we had was one 20 pound bag of rice and barley. The six of us remaining in Seoul (mother, sister, three boys and Grandmother Young Wha Kim) ate as little as possible—a thin gruel of rice and barley—so that we could stretch our food supply and prolong our existence. We had no idea how long Seoul would be occupied by the communists or whether we could resist surrendering indefinitely. We had been cut off from any communication from our father for some time. We worried about his safety and wondered where he was. Seoul was a huge metropolitan city with a population of ten million or so. Many went underground to evade apprehension by the North Korean soldiers. The communist police were hunting for those who escaped from North Korea as they saw them as traitors. They were also arresting South Korean civic and political leaders, professors and intellectuals. They rounded up all young men and any "serviceable and usable" citizens. The communists were desperately searching everyplace for young adults whom they could draft into their North Korean Army. Young adult males were being picked up on a massive scale and drafted into the North Korean Army. I decided to hide underground to avoid detection by the North Korean authorities. As a hiding place, I made a shape of coffin-like space under the closet wooden floor by cutting a hole in the closet wooden floor and digging some dirt soil underneath so that I could enter and exit from the hiding space. After I crawled down to the hiding space, my sister would cover the entry hole of the closet floor with a big cardboard box containing clothes. When I needed to come out of the hiding space, I used to yell for my sister so that she could remove the cardboard box.

In the afternoon of August 27, 1950, two civilian clothed men came to our house and asked for my mother. Whenever someone came to our house, I would quickly slip into my hiding place under the closet floor. From under the floor I could still hear people talking above me. I was hiding because I was a college student and the right age for being conscripted into the North Korean Army. When the two men came to our house, I ran and hid under the floor. My youngest brother Ik Poong went to the door to greet them. They asked for my mother and Ik Poong told them that she was not home at the moment. They did not try to enter the house. One of them told my brother that they had some news from our father in the south, and that they would be back the following day to talk to our mother about the news. They emphasized to Ik Poong, "Make sure that your mother waits for us when we come back tomorrow, about at this time!"

My mother was happy and excited with the prospect that she would finally hear news from our father through his friends. She waited and waited until the following day, thinking that the two men were father's friends. They showed up at the door as they promised. I could not trust them myself, so I again hid in my coffin box under the floor. Mother dashed to the door to welcome them. My brother Ik Sung was behind mother and heard them say that they needed a quieter place to talk and asked her to follow them outside. She followed them and they walked down the alley which leads to the asphalt street. After waiting a few minutes, I felt very uneasy. I came out from my hiding place and told my sister Ik Nan and brothers to go outside and see what they were doing with our mother in the street. They went outside and searched, but could not find them anywhere. They returned crying and in a panic shouting "They are gone! They are gone!" My sister and the brothers went out again and looked all over the neighborhood. They asked our neighbors if they had seen our mother and they said no. Out of desperation, my sister, naively, went as far as to the Seodai Moon prison (West Gate prison) in Seoul and describing mother's appearance asked the prison guard if they had seen her coming through the gate. Later a young boy told us that he saw a car waiting in the street and two men put our mother inside the car and drove away. That was the last time we saw her. The date of mother's kidnap was August 28, 1950.

It has been more than 60 years since our mother was taken by the communist secret agents! We have not heard from her, nor received any news or information as to whether she is alive or dead, and her whereabouts if she is alive. We made our full effort to seek out any information about mother using various channels, including the Joint International Red Cross Team. We learned later that hundreds and hundreds of Korean leaders in different professional fields were kidnapped in South Korea and put in prison by the same method used on our mother. Later when Seoul was about to be recaptured by U.N. forces, the kidnapped prisoners were forced to march on foot to North Korea. Most likely, my mother was imprisoned and then taken to North Korea in one of these forced marches. These kidnapped prisoners were forced to walk up to 200 miles on foot, and those who became weak or sick dropped dead or were shot to death if they walked too slowly. Most likely our mother died, and we will probably never learn where or when she died. If she were alive today, she would be 106 years old. We think that she was arrested because she was an active leader in a Christian women's organization in Seoul.

[3-4] Escape to Buyo: Following the kidnapping and disappearance of our mother, we were very afraid, if we were to remain in Seoul, of being apprehended and drafted into the North Korean Army. Moreover, our food supply was running out. The occupying communist forces had totally blockaded and barricaded Seoul, preventing foods and other merchandise from being delivered into the city. It was a matter of only two or three weeks before Seoul's entire food supply would be depleted. People were beginning to starve. The streets of Seoul were noisy with blaring announcements coming from the loud speakers mounted on North Korean Army trucks. The speaker would shout: "Comrades, welcome to the bosom of our Fatherland. Come to us, and we will give you food and work." Many people in households with little or no food reserves came out and gave up to the North Korean Army. As a result of this forced

surrender, so many "serviceable" young adults were involuntarily drafted into the North Korean Army.

At this juncture, my two younger brothers and I had to flee Seoul; there was no food left in the house and no way to buy or otherwise secure food. Leaving our 70 years old paternal grandmother Young Hwa Kim and younger sister Ik Nan (18 years old) behind in our house in Seoul, we disguised ourselves and managed to slip out of Seoul. Not knowing exactly where to go, we walked on foot toward Buyo which is an ancient city from the Shilla Dynasty (3rd-6th AD). We had been told that we had distant relatives living in Buyo and so we decided to head there. On the way through rural country, we were stopped from time to time by North Korean military personnel. We passed their scrutiny each time by presenting counterfeit communist official documents which were prepared for me by a friend who had some connections in the Communist Party. We became bolder as we became hungrier. A couple times on the way, we went to a local Communist Party office and introduced ourselves with our official documents and informed them that we were on the way to the battle line with a specific mission. They provided food and lodging for us twice. At that time, telephone communication lines were primitive and almost non-existent. Luckily the North Koreans were unable to verify our documents with their headquarters. We finally reached a rural area near Buyo where our distant relatives lived and we stayed with them.

On September 28, 1950 we heard that Seoul had been recaptured after a successful surprise amphibious landing under General Douglas MacArthur's command in Inchon Harbor west of Seoul. Following that landing, the U.N. forces pushed toward Seoul and then advanced across the 38th parallel continuing north as far as the Yalu River bordering with China. After the U.N. forces secured Seoul, my brothers and I returned from Buyo. We found out that while we were away from Seoul, our maternal grandmother passed away during the North Korean Army occupation.

[3-5] My service as an interpreter in ROK Army Intelligence Unit: Upon returning to Seoul, I met a friend who was a Republic of Korea (ROK) Army lieutenant who recommended that I apply for an interpreter position in the ROK Army Intelligence Unit. I applied and I passed a rather rigorous written examination in English. With only a brief orientation and no other training, I was ordered and dispatched

to Hamhung, a major industrial city in North Korea. Just east of Hamhung is the port of Hungnam which faces the East Sea. Five of us in the ROK Army Intelligence Unit were put on a U.S. Air Force airplane. We landed in Hamhung which had been recently captured. We were not informed of our mission at the time. I later learned that we were scheduled to go behind enemy lines as a special intelligence unit to conduct spy activities. It was a secret and clandestine operation. None of our unit members were told about it. My ulterior motive in joining the Intelligence Unit was, in my vague way of thinking, to seek out any news of our kidnapped mother.

The battle situation changed rapidly. When I was stationed in North Korea for a week or so, the U.N. and South Korea forces had already advanced rapidly deep into the northern part of North Korea, almost reaching the Yalu River which borders China. As the South Korean and U.N. forces marched further into North Korea, they were enthusiastically welcomed by large numbers of North Korean people, who ran to them, waving flags and cheering. They had gotten tired of the miserable hardship and intolerable oppression of living under the North Korea communist regime. These North Koreans welcomed and aligned themselves with the U.N. forces, but their joy was short-lived. Soon the Chinese military became engaged in the Korean War and the Korean peoples' dreams and hopes for unification and peace were destroyed.

[3-6] Involvement of the Chinese Volunteer Army:
Mao Tse Tung of Communist China reacted swiftly and decided to intervene in the Korean War with more than 300,000 Communist Chinese soldiers, so called the "Chinese Volunteer Army." The fighting took a sharp turnabout. The Chinese Volunteer Army (hereafter called the Chinese Communist Army) marched secretly by night with rifles on their shoulders. By the time U.N. headquarters learned about this situation, the Chinese military had already encircled the U.N. forces, especially U.S. Marine Corps, in the Chongjin area. Like an army of ants, the Chinese Communist Army overwhelmed the U.N. forces by their sheer numbers. The U.N. forces had to retreat and evacuate from North Korea on a massive scale. They faced the fierce counter-attack by the "countless human sea" of the Chinese Communist Army.

It was a bitter December winter with snow, blizzards and subzero temperatures, so cold that it was said a stream of urine would freeze before hitting the ground. The narrow, snowy road in between steep mountains where the U.N. forces were moving was a perfect target for Chinese fire power. Hundreds of U.S. Marines were trapped while in retreat and killed on this "death road" by the barrage of Chinese heavy artillery. The U.S. military tried to evacuate its 4,000 wounded soldiers by building a temporary airport. Otherwise, they had to walk, marching day and night for 44 miles. Some of the American soldiers had never experienced such cold and snow. Many of the wounded froze to death while being pulled on sleds by fellow soldiers over the snowy ground.

[3-7] Hungnam Evacuation: As the large numbers of U.N. forces were retreating to the Hungnam area, General MacArthur ordered about 200 U.S. Navy warships and merchant marine freighter/cargo ships to assemble in the Hungnam harbor ready for a massive evacuation operation, "historically the largest evacuation by sea in maritime military history according to the Guinness Book of Records, the "Hungnam Evacuation."

The U.N. forces had been so confident that they could drive straight through to the North without any resistance that they had brought in 17,500 military vehicles and tanks, as well as 357 tons of food and military supplies to the Chongjin area. The retreating U.N. forces could not leave behind tanks and cannons. The U.S. military authorities were primarily preoccupied with strategic plans to transport U.S. military personnel and their equipment out of Korea. Their first priority was to put on board about 100,000 military personnel and heavy military equipment, vehicles and tanks. Artillery and heavy weapons were burned and fiercely destroyed by the 10th Army so as not to fall into the enemy hands of the rapidly advancing Chinese Communist Army.

Along with the retreating U.N. forces, thousands and thousands of North Koreans refugees began pouring into Hungnam Harbor where they waited hoping to board one of the 200 ships. It was a chaotic scene with many refugees—both older people, younger women, and women heavily burdened with babies on their backs, holding the hands of younger children, and balancing luggage on their heads—all fighting each other to get on a ship.

Until then, U.N. authorities had not thought of and therefore did not plan on the possibility that they might have to accommodate the North Korean refugees aboard ship. They were also concerned with the ships' safety and security with so many civilian citizens of the enemy country they were actively fighting against. Meanwhile, the North Korean refugees would not leave the harbor even briefly because they had no way of knowing when the ships would depart, so they endured the bitter winter cold as best as they could.

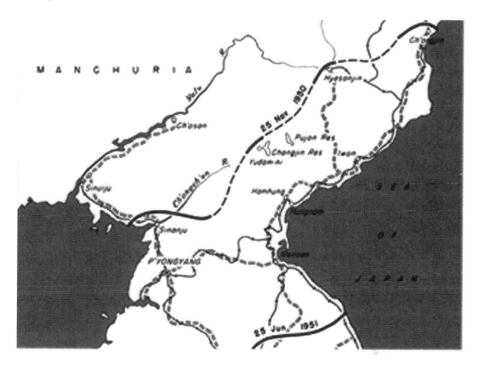

Chongjin Reservoir area in the Regional map of North Korea

North Korean refugees going toward Hungnam to be rescued
North Korean refugees at Hungnam waiting to be picked up by the US transport ships (December 12, 1950)

[3-8] Dr. Bonghak Hyun's crucial role on rescuing NK refugees:

Dr. Bonghak Hyun was a graduate of Yonsei Medical School, a professor of pathology at Thomas Jefferson University Medical School and a personal advisor and friend of General Edward M (Ned) Almond, Commander of the X Corps of the 8th Army. Dr. Hyun approached General Almond, urging him to allow the North Korean refugees to board ship. He emphasized to General Almond, "The Communists would not forget that these North Koreans refugees had enthusiastically welcomed and took sides with U.N. forces. These people would be imprisoned and some group leaders would likely be put to death. I can vouch that these North Koreans who welcomed the U.N. forces are not Communists because I know them well enough; they include my relatives, friends of my relatives and my own hometown old friends."

General Almond was reluctant and at first he turned down Dr. Hyun's request. It was reported that President Syngman Rhee himself and some ROK Army generals also appealed and urged General Almond not to abandon, but rescue the North Korean refugees by allowing them to get on board the U.S. ships. Dr. Hyun persisted in asking General Almond to permit North Korean refugees to board. The situation became such that the U.N. forces could not delay their retreat any longer and, at the last moment, General Almond finally authorized North Korean refugees to board putting them in whatever space was available between cannons and tanks and elsewhere on the ships. I feel that Dr. Hyun's persistent effort to persuade General Almond with his personal appeals rescued the North Korean refugees.

Photo of Dr Bong Hak Hyun who rescued North Korean refugees by persuading Gen. Almond to allow to aboard ships

[3-9] My serving as a transport ship captain's interpreter:

While I was trying to get onboard a U.S. Navy transport ship myself, the ship's captain needed a Korean interpreter to announce his orders and instructions in Korean over the ship's public announcement (PA) system. The captain asked me to be his interpreter, a duty of which I gladly accepted.

By the time I boarded, there were already thousands of U.N. personnel including ROK Army soldiers in the bunk beds. The North Korean refugees were in between tanks and vehicles and whatever space was available on the interior floors of the ship. On deck refugees were jam-packed like canned sardines. The refugees had to cling to each other to prevent from being blown off deck by the strong cold winds. As the ship approached rough, choppy sea, many refugees became seasick and at times there was noise and some commotion among the frightened and confused North Koreans. Small children were crying. On board the captain communicated his messages, announcements and warnings through the ship's PA system which could be heard throughout the ship. I translated the captain's words, sentence by sentence, into Korean so that ROK soldiers and North Korean refugees could understand his messages. I slept in a room next to the captain's room. I followed him wherever he went around the ship and translated questions and answers for the Korean-speaking.

After the evacuation, the final report of the captain stated that the North Korean refugees were generally cooperative and disciplined and followed the captain's instructions without any reportable incident in the three day voyage from Hungnam to Koje-Do Island near Busan. According to the historical archives of the U.S. Defense Department, altogether 100,000 U.S. soldiers, tanks, military vehicles and close to 100,000 North Korean refugees were evacuated from Hungnam within the span of a few days and transported safely to Koje-Do Island by approximately 110 participating U.S. Navy and Merchant Marine ships.

North Koreans waiting for LST boats which take them to the US cargo ships anchored at several miles away. Soldiers trying to get down from the cargo ships to LST boats.

[3-10] The Ship of Miracles:

One of the cargo ships, the *SS Meredith Viceroy* with a maximum capacity of 1,400 had loaded and transported 14,000 refugees on board. This was 10 times over the ship's capacity; it was truly a miracle that the ship stayed afloat and did not sink. I believe that special recognition has been given to the S.S. Meredith Victory's participation in the Hungnam Evacuation primarily as result of the publication of *Ship of Miracles* by Bill Gilbert, whose extensive interviews and research provided solid documentation of that ship's role. Gilbert was formerly a Washington Post reporter and also a Korean War veteran of the U.S. Air Force. In *Ship of Miracles*, Gilbert describes the real-life courage of loading and safely transporting the 14,000 North Korean refugees, the humanitarian spirit shown by its crew members, as well as the amazing story of Captain Leonard LaRue, who was spiritually transformed through the experience. Subsequent to his discharge from marine duty, LaRue became a Catholic monk and spent the rest of his life in a New Jersey monastery.

Ship of Miracles also documented that during the S.S. Meredith Victory's voyage, five Korean babies were born. Luckily, there was an experienced Korean midwife among the refugees who delivered all the babies in a competent manner.

I am glad that among the U.S. merchant marine ships participating in Hungnam Evacuation, the S.S. Meredith Victory has been singularly recognized with a special citation and honored with a display of a life size monument of the S.S. Meredith Victory at Koje-Do Island. Recognition is also due to all other U.S. military and transport/cargo ships that rescued North Korean refugees in this evacuation.

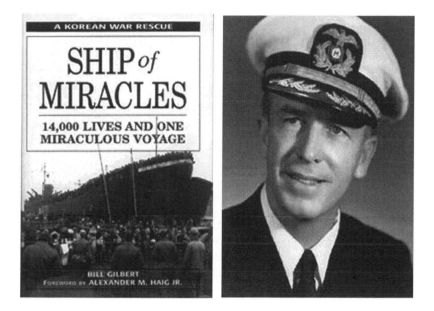

Captain of the SS Meredith Victory, Leonard La Rue. Book cover "Ship of Miracles" referring to S.S. Meredith Victory.

Jam-packed Korean refugees on the deck of SS Meredith Victory.

[3-11] R.J. McHatton, video producer: A well-known
video producer, Mr. R.J. McHatton of Seattle, Washington, was so moved and inspired by the story of the *Ship of Miracles* that he personally financed the production of a video documentary "The Ship of Miracles: the Hungnam Evacuation." Mr. McHatton met Dr. Hyun Bonghak who told him about my involvement in the Hungnam Evacuation. When Mr. McHatton contacted me, he asked for help locating U.S. Korean War veterans and North Korean refugees who were present in the evacuation and wanted me to recruit anyone who was willing to be interviewed for the documentary. At the time my wife Grace was president of the Korean American Community Association of Greater Sacramento and she publicized in English and Korean newspapers seeking anyone who personally experienced the evacuation. We were able to find several veterans and three Korean American ladies in the Sacramento area and arranged Mr. McHatton to interview them. According to Mr. McHatton, the completed video documentary will be shown nationally.

In the documentary's last scene showing a crowd of North Korean refugees commemorating the Koje-Do monument of S.S. Meredith Victory, you can hear the song "Yearning for My Home" which I composed and was sung by Jaeho Lee, M.D., a tenor opera singer and friend of mine in Sacramento. The final scene with choral singing of *Arirang,* a traditional Korean folk song, was performed by the Sacramento Korean American Choral Society which was founded by Grace. Mr. McHatton was kind to dedicate his documentary to the memory of my kidnapped mother Woon Bong Choo. He has become a close friend of ours and completed a video autobiography of Grace's and my life, part of which was shown on YouTube under the title of "Luke & Grace Kim Trailer."

(Left to right) Luke, Grace, Paul Kim (youngest brother), and R J McHartton (video producer), far right side, visiting my home.

[3-12] Impact of the Hungnam Evacuation on my life:

My experience of the Hungnam Evacuation impacted my subsequent spiritual growth and life philosophy. I believe the difficult evacuation was possible primarily due to the humanitarian spirit of the American soldiers and sailors which led them to load, transport and lead to freedom so many North Korean civilian refugees on their ships. I also believe that the emotional bonding among the family members, friends and Korean neighbors and acquaintances, and among Korean people, namely *jeong*-feelings provided the spirit of belonging and mutual support among Korean people and important energy to persevere, survive and overcome despite enormous adversity. The Korean word *jeong* is similar to the Korean/Asian concept of "love" representing the union of "we, togetherness." In contrast, the Western concept of love emphases the individual 'I.' (Further discussion on *jeong* is in Chapter 6, subtitle 6-12 "Introducing Korean Ethos," and the full text of my article on Korean Ethos is in the Appendix),

More recently, on March 12, 2011, there was a special occasion to celebrate and commemorate the 60th anniversary of the Hungnam Evacuation in an event called "Korean War Tribute Day aboard the S.S. Lane Victory." It was held at San Pedro, California where the S.S. Lane Victory was berthed. The S.S. Lane Victory is the only Hungnam Evacuation merchant cargo ship remaining and still in use out of the hundred-plus similar merchant cargo ships that transported North Korean refugees safely to Koje Island.

On my behalf, Grace gave a brief talk on the Hungnam Evacuation to the audience gathered there to celebrate in San Pedro. Mr. McHatton flew down for the event to introduce his final version of the "Ship of Miracles." The documentary was popular and well received and many people purchased the DVD that day. Mr. McHatton plans to release the DVD for sale to the public.

Koreans worship General Douglas MacArthur (statue located in Inchon Korea).

Chapter 4

Refugee Life In Busan (1951-1953)

[4-1] My return to Seoul and our family's train ride on the roof top to Busan: After I finished my duties as an interpreter, I got off the U.S. transport ship at a small fishing village on the east coast of South Korea. In the meantime, we received orders from ROK Army Headquarters that our Intelligence Unit was disbanded and the non-commissioned, civilian interpreter/intelligence agents are free to leave on their own without a need for further reporting. Our former ROK Army Intelligence Unit members got on a military truck and headed for Seoul. The roads were tortuous going around and around, ascending and descending big mountains. Finally, we arrived in Seoul.

I reunited with my family after about one month of separation. In the meantime, the North Korean Army and Chinese Communist Army advanced south crossing the 38th parallel and recaptured Seoul. Waves and waves of refugees were trying to get out of Seoul again before the communist forces closed in and sealed off the city. Our family—father, my sister, two brothers and I were among the massive numbers of refugees trying to escape from Seoul.

The train was overcrowded and everybody was struggling and shoving each other to get on the train. After much pushing and being pushed, we were lucky to catch the very last freight train leaving Seoul heading south toward Busan, a harbor city on the southern tip of South Korea. The freight cars were already jam packed full of people, like sardines in a can. We climbed on top of a freight car rooftop and situated ourselves there. Even on the roofs, people were fighting for sitting spots. Whenever the train went through tunnels, we had to lower our heads and hold onto each other and we felt hot, black smokes hitting our faces. Our faces became more and more blackened with smoke each time we passed through tunnels. The train would stop and go capriciously as if the train wanted to move whenever it felt like it. It took almost two and one half days to reach Busan, which was no more than 300 miles from Seoul.

On the way, the train would stop at small village stations. One time, my sister tried to get down from the freight car roof to go to the station's restroom. Halfway down, she slipped and fell down to the ground as her hands and feet were so cold and almost frozen that she had lost the sensation of griping. She passed out for a couple of minutes, and I tried hard to revive her. Luckily she came to her senses and went to the restroom. I helped her climb back up to the roof before the train began to leave.

When we arrived at Busan, we had no money nor places to stay. We were literally homeless for three weeks. We slept outdoors with blankets in the front yard of the Cho-Riang Presbyterian Church, gazing at the bright stars in the clear winter sky. I was lucky and found a day-wage job at the Busan dock. It was hard labor work unloading heavy sacks or boxes of military supplies from the conveyer and carrying them on my shoulder to the trucks. At the end of each day, I was paid my small wage of $3.50 for the day's work. I would stop by a fish market and buy a small bag of rice and a dozen pieces of squid, which was the cheapest sea food. My family waited for me to return with groceries as they did not have any food all day. We cooked rice and squid on an outdoor fire and ate the so tasty food happily. To this day squid is my favorite dish. Whenever I eat squid now, I can smell the unique aroma of the squid that we cooked and ate while living as refugees in Busan.

[4-2] Our refugee life at the Yongdo Buddhist Temple refugee camp in Busan: Later we were able to secure and move to a spot in a refugee camp located at the Yongdo Buddhist Temple. There were already about 100 refugee families living there. We pitched a 6 x 10 foot tent, and five of us lived in that tent for the next two years. There was no electricity. We cooked food over a charcoal fire outside the tent and used a kerosene lamp as a light source during the night. It was almost impossible for anyone to read books for more than 15 minutes with the limited light provided by the kerosene lamp. The Yongdo refugee camp did not have plumbing nor any toilet sanitary system. There was no water supply system either and we had to scoop tiny amounts of water every morning from the only well available in the camp. At three or four o'clock in the morning, people were already standing in a long line in front of the well in order to get some water. The amount of water seeping up through the bottom of the ten foot deep well was so tiny that my father had to lower a bucket and scoop the water from the bottom of the well more than 30-50 times to get about 5 gallons of water. People stood in line for their turn to get water for hours. We used the water for cooking, and any leftover was used for washing our faces. It was a miracle that none of us got sick in the refugee camp. During those two years I left earlier to join the Korean Navy.

[4-3] My enlisting with the Korean Navy: One day while I was in the Yongdo refugee camp, I read a newspaper advertisement stating that the Korean Navy was recruiting those who were studying medicine at a medical school, but not yet graduated, as well as those who were pre-medical students to enlist with the Korean Navy as hospital corpsmen. I had been in the ROK Army Intelligence Unit which was neither a commissioned nor enlisted position, but a civilian appointment attached to the Army Intelligence Unit. I felt that I needed to serve the country somehow, so I considered active military service and applied to be a Navy hospital corpsman. As part of the application process, I took an examination evaluating my medical knowledge with questions like "Describe the pathologies of the pancreas." I had to answer such questions on pathology with common sense knowledge because I had not attended medical school yet. Somehow, I passed the exam, though one of my Seoul High School classmates took the same exam and did not pass.

After receiving basic boot camp training and paramedical training for altogether four months, I was given the rank of a third class petty officer, a ranking based on my level of medical education. For example, if I were in the first year class of medical school, I would have been given the rank of a "first class petty officer." I became a third class petty officer hospital corpsman because I was only a pre-med student.

I was selected and sent to the U.S. Navy hospital ships anchored at Busan, namely the Repose and the Consolation. On board I went through four months of training in the clinical laboratory. I learned how to run laboratory tests on blood, urine and stool. I also learned how to do lab work looking for parasites under the microscope. After completing this lab training, I was assigned to the Korean Naval Hospital in Chinhae where I ran the medical laboratory. I became a lab specialist in parasitology because an increasing number of Korean military personnel had parasites in their GI systems.

Luke Kim, 3rd class petty officer Korean Navy, Summer 1951

Luke Kim Korean Navy days.

Now the Korean War had come to a stalemate. The U.N. forces and communists were fighting in a seesaw way, retreating from and retaking strategic positions back and forth in the bunkers during the nights along the 38th Parallel. In this slow, murderous fighting process, huge casualties were suffered, especially the Korean Marine Corps which had many wounded soldiers. I was scheduled to be transferred from the Korean Navy to the Korean Marine Corps (KMC) to take care of wounded soldiers and was ordered to report to the Korean Marine Corps (KMC) Headquarters in Busan. When I did, they assigned me to the KMC personnel desk in the KMC Medical Department, an office assignment instead of nursing duties taking care of wounded soldiers at a military hospital which I expected. I later heard that they chose me for the personnel office because supposedly I had a reputation for writing good official letters and having good penmanship.

[4-4] Discharge from the military to go back to medical school: In the meantime, war casualties were increasing and the South Korean government and military forces were in urgent need of more medical doctors. By government order, I was discharged early from the Korean Marine Corps after only one year and ten months of active military service to complete my medical education. In 1951, I return to Seoul National University (SNU) and enrolled at SNU Medical School to study medicine and in 1956 received my M.D. degree.

In looking back, I wonder how we were able to study medicine under such poor wartime conditions. We were still in the middle of the Korean War and all of the SNU school buildings in Seoul were occupied by North Korean and Chinese Communist Armies. Our "medical school" was a temporary canvas-pitched tent classroom in Busan. Classroom instruction consisted mainly of the professor's lectures with his anatomic structure drawings on a blackboard and poor mimeographed copies of diagrams of the human anatomy. We did not have medical textbooks nor any reference/ resource books. That is why to this day, I still tend to horde and am reluctant to give away anatomy textbooks with richly colored drawings and colorful photos that I missed so very much during my medical school days.

My father was unemployed, we had no income, I could not afford to pay my medical school tuition and there were no scholarships in those days. I am forever grateful to my younger sister Ik Nan who sacrificially suspended her own college education in order to help support the family by working as a bank teller and later as a school clerk; Ik Nan put me through medical school by paying my tuition. She was admitted to Ewha Women's University as fine arts major just prior to the outbreak of the Korean War. She resumed her college art education some years after I completed my medical school and she got married.

Through intense battles, Seoul changed hands three times between the opposing forces. In the process, Seoul was totally destroyed and pulverized. The fighting gradually fell into a standstill, with no win situation for either side. On the battlefront, casualties continued to remain high without either side making any headway. Armistice negotiations between North Korean and the U.N. commanders were held at the 38th parallel near Panmunjum. After considerable maneuvering and tough negotiations by both sides for more than two years, on July 27, 1953 an armistice agreement was finally reached ending the bitter warfare.

I heard about many episodes of ridiculous, playful and yet serious maneuvering tactics displayed during the armistice negotiation meetings. One example is that while arranging the room and getting ready for the meeting, a North Korean military person would inconspicuously make their extendable flag stand on the table slightly taller than the height of the U.N. flag displayed on our side of the table. Recognizing this, the U.N. person would make the U.N. flag slightly taller than the North Korean flag before the meeting started. Both sides kept trying to out do each other by raising the height of their respective flags each time before the meeting started. Both flags were finally displayed so conspicuously high on the table that everyone chuckled.

With Ik San Kim (left), one of my Seoul High and medical school classmates and a close friend who suffered from bipolar disorder while in med school. However, later he became a successful surgeon practicing in South Africa. I became interested in psychiatry because of him (photo taken in military fatigue Uniform in 1953)

[4-5] My summer job as a secretary/interpreter with the Joint International Red Cross Team:

In the summer of 1953, I was a third year medical student looking for a summer job. After quite rigorous and competitive job interviews, I was selected and had a rare, unique and very interesting opportunity for a three month summer job with the Office of Secretariat of the Joint International Red Cross Team.

The Joint Armistice Commission gave the Joint International Red Cross Team the task and responsibility of monitoring compliance with mutually agreed upon protocols for the repatriation of prisoners of war (POWs) once the ceasefire began. The Red Cross Team was to directly observe and supervise the repatriation process at the 38th Parallel. The Team was composed of representatives of the United States, Denmark, Australia, Philippines, England, and other countries.

The Joint International Red Cross Team of both sides combined at Panmunjom, far right is Luke Kim (1953).

Left-side photo: Luke Kim as a secretary/interpreter for the International Red Cross Team whose task was to supervise POWs' exchange at the make-shift building (left photo) located at 38th parallel near Panmunjom where negotiating meetings take place (1953).

Right-side photo: Tent station of the Joint International Red Cross Team just above the 38th parallel where North Korean-returning POWs lined up complaining of inhumane treatment by UN authority while in POW camp. Front standing is Luke Kim.

The above photo is the scene where North Korean soldiers returning to North Korea threw away newly issued uniform, by shouting, "This dirty Yankee clothes, I don't need them." But then it was found that they threw away clothes and boots just after they pass of the North of 38th parallel, not before. Following morning, street was clean and clear because they picked up the clothes and the boots during the night.

I accompanied the Joint International Red Cross Team very early in the morning to observe and supervise the POW exchanges. We flew by helicopter to the tent station temporarily set up immediately north of the 38th Parallel for the returning North Korean and Chinese POWs. There was a separate tent station temporarily set up just south of the 38th Parallel for returning U.N. and South Korean POWs.

We made comical yet sad observations at the exchange point. As truckloads of North Korean prisoners were driven toward the exchange station, they were waving their fists, shouting "Down with Yankees!" and singing their military songs. As the trucks were driving through the check-point, the returning North Korean prisoners began to disrobe, layer by layer, throwing down to the ground their recently issued green military uniforms and shoes from the truck. Many of them became almost naked except for shorts. They shouted, "These dirty Yankee clothes; we don't need them!" Interestingly, they threw these clothes only after the truck passed through and was within the North Korean communist zone and not before. When we returned to the same site the next day, the new clothes and shoes were all picked up by the North Korean soldiers and the roads were clean and clear. After observing the scene, a Filipino representative of the Joint International Red Cross Team grinned and sarcastically said, "They seem to know what they are doing."

During the POW exchange, we observed that when the returning North Korean prisoners were turned over to the North Korean receiving officer they displayed highly emotionally charged and spirited behaviors and it was a very politicized event. The returning North Korean POWs went through a ceremonial ritual: the receiving officer would salute the prisoners and say, "We welcome our comrades. Welcome to the bosom of our Fatherland." Then the prisoners would respond with loud shouts of "*Mansei* (long life) to the People's Republic of Korea! *Mansei* to our great leader Kim IL Sung! "They shouted loudly and acted in high spirits. They all looked healthy and energetic. On the other hand, when the U.N. and South Korean prisoners were turned over to the South Korean side, many of them were somber, silent and/or sobbed or crying with happy emotions. They looked tired, haggard and emaciated. I overheard a U.S. war correspondent asking an American prisoner how he felt and what he wanted to know most about what was going on in the United States. The soldier asked him "How is Marilyn Monroe doing these days?" Another soldier asked, "What is the score of the New York Yankees?" I thought to myself what a difference and contrast! The North Korean POWs were completely indoctrinated and ordered to behave as political puppets, while the American prisoners were behaving as natural and "apolitical" human beings.

While we were observing and supervising the exchange process, the North Korean POWs formed a long line in the tent station and wanted to talk to our Red Cross Team one by one. They filed complaints verbally or in writing alleging inhumane treatment while they were incarcerated as prisoners by the Americans. They wanted to show us signs of their physical malaise, scars, malnutrition, chemical poisoning and so forth as evidence of maltreatment. They insisted that the Red Cross Team document each and every one of their complaints and their evidence of cruelty. As part of the duties assigned to the Red Cross Team, we documented each POW complaints and I translated their complaints in Korean to English. Their complaints were almost exactly the same as if they memorized what they were told to report. The North Korean POWs demanded that the Joint International Red Cross Team investigate and confirm that, "the American authority treated POWs cruelly while incarcerated, based on the testimonies given by the returning North Korean POWs."

In a subsequent Joint International Red Cross team meeting consisting of the Red cross representatives of both sides, the communist representatives proposed that based on what they saw and heard from the returning North Korean and Chinese prisoners, the Joint International Red Cross team must declare to the whole world that the Red Cross Team found evidence of inhumane treatment and cruelty suffered by North Korean POWs at the hands of U.N. prison guards while the North Koreans were held in prison. It was a very tense moment and a very emotionally charged scene to say the least. Finally, the Red Cross Team members from our side responded that the statements of the North Korean POWs were politically indoctrinated, manipulated acts, and far from reality. Then the Red Cross Team of our side walked out together from that meeting which was the last activity of the Joint International Red Cross Team.

The South Korean representative of the Joint International Red Cross Team was Mr. Bumsuk Lee. I worked closely with Mr. Lee during that summer job as a secretary/interpreter for the Red Cross Team. Later on Mr. Lee told me that he met with President Syngman Rhee and reported to him everything that was going on at the POW exchange point and his final analysis of what happened with the Joint International Red Cross Team. He told me that President Rhee expressed his appreciation of Mr. Lee's contributions and participation in the important assignment he had as the South Korean representative to the Red Cross Team.

In subsequent years, Mr. Bumsuk Lee was appointed to be the Minister of Foreign Affairs in the cabinet of President Doo Whan Chun, Republic of Korea. During an official tour of President Chun with an entourage of cabinet ministers, secretaries and reporters to Langoon, the capital city of Myanmar (formerly Burma), a North Korean terrorists group placed a time bomb at the ceremonial platform prior to an official ceremony. While the presidential party waited on the platform and just before President Chun's arrival, the bomb exploded killing 17 members of the presidential team, including the Minister of Finance, the president's Chief's Economic Advisor, and Mr. Bumsuk Lee. The North Korean terrorists were apprehended several days later. I would like here to express my deep condolence to his family for the most untimely death of the honorable Bumsuk Lee, Minister of Foreign Affairs, Republic of Korea.

During this summer job with the Joint International Red Cross Team, I attempted to find the whereabouts of my mother through Red Cross channels. The North Korean government stonewalled and I could not get any information. In 1987, through an informal but reliable connection with the North Korean Government, my brother Ik Poong also attempted to find out if our mother was still alive in North Korea. He never received a satisfactory answer, and it is assumed that his contact could not locate her. Probably she was already dead.

Chapter 5

Family Life after the Korean War (1953-1962)

[5-1] Meeting Miss Chun Kyung Ja (전경자,田敬子), my future wife Grace: While a refugee in Busan, I met Miss Chun Kyung Ja for the first time at the Hyup-Dong-Kwan (Cooperation House). At Hyup-Dong-Kwan center, college students got together to study the Bible and discuss Christianity. Bible study was under the guidance of Oh Ki Hyung, a professor at Yonsei University. We not only studied the Bible but also performed community service. In those days, college boys and girls did not date or associate with each other closely, even if they liked each other inwardly.

After returning to Seoul from Busan, I attended the Youngnak Presbyterian Church. In the meanwhile Kyung Ja had also returned to Seoul and we kept in contact. I continued to meet her at the Hyup-Dong-Kwan in Seoul, but then we were still not "dating." One evening at the Hyup-Dong-Kwan (Cooperation House) located near the Seoul National University College of Liberal Arts and Science, Kyung Ja asked me to escort her to the bus station because it was a very dark evening. I accepted her request gladly. We talked while walking to the bus station, which turned out to be our "first date."

My future wife Grace (Miss Kyung Ja Chun) in 1952

To me, Kyung Ja had, and still has, stunning beauty, a special kind of beauty with purity and nobility, and a very sociable, pleasant, outgoing personality which attracted lots of attention from many men. Therefore, my heart quivered when I accepted her request to escort her to the bus station that evening. Her older brother Sang Wan Chun, who later became a minister at the Presbyterian Church USA, used to chaperon her constantly until then.

She said that she used to say "no" automatically to any men trying to approach and ask her for date, regardless circumstances and who the person might be. It was lucky for me that, while her brother was hospitalized in SNU hospital where I used to visit him, I had the opportunity to get to know her better.

In spite of quite different birth place (Grace in Shanghai China, and I myself in North Korea), we discovered that we come from a similar background of Christian faith, service- oriented life style, and life goal: the importance of education and role model as a teacher, mentor and a community activist leader, advocating social justice and protecting the interest of the poor, weak, voiceless and powerless as the underdog of society.

One day I suggested going to see the opera "Carmen" with her, but she said, "No." When I insisted, she finally accepted my invitation. We dated for about one year or so until I decided to go abroad to study in the United States. About three months prior to my departure for America, I made my proposal to her. Before making a decision, she suggested consulting with Professor Kim Suk Mok whom both of us respected highly. Professor Kim said that since I was going to be too far away for an unknown period of time, it was not advisable to be engaged. "But when the time comes, you can marry if both of you still love each other." We agreed to the professor's suggestion and decided not to become engaged to each other. Later we learned that both of us were convinced that we would eventually be married no matter how long it would take.

Family Photo in 1954, back from left to right: Ik Sung Ik Chang (Luke), Father, Ik Poong, front from left: Grandmother, Step-mother

[5-2] Family Members

[5-3] New stepmother Kim Young Ja: After my mother
was kidnapped, my father worked hard to support the family by himself.
After our family and relatives returned to Seoul, we had a family council
and advised my father to remarry.

"Father, you have gone through all sorts of hardships. Please consider
a remarriage."

"No, I'll never marry again."

My father stubbornly resisted the idea, but all the children and relatives
continued to persuade him to remarry.

"Father, this house needs a mother who can help you, so that each of
us can go our own way."

Upon our insistence, my father finally accepted the idea of remarriage
and decided to remarry. Dr. Kim Yun Soo MD (Ik Nan's future father-in-law)
introduced father to Kim Young Ja whose birthdate is November 11, 1907
and who ran an orphanage in Hae-woon-dae near Busan. She was a graduate
of the Christian Girl's High School in P'yongyang and when she moved to
Seoul, worked at the Korean Women's Association. Her background was
similar to that of our birth mother. After Kim Young Ja's marriage to our
father, she took pretty good care of our family, especially the youngest, Ik
Poong (Paul), so he was very attached to her.

In 1976, father and his wife had a six-month visit to the United States
and returned to Korea. Later, at my invitation, in July, 1978, both of
them decided to come to the United States as immigrants and they lived
in Sacramento, California about thirty minutes driving distance from our
home in Davis. My father was an Elder and my stepmother a Deaconess
in the Sacramento Korean Church. My father used to visit sick church
members by bicycle. My stepmother attended English class in adult school
and won an award for perfect attendance for two years. My father traveled
to Davis by bus once or twice a week and used to clean our swimming pool
as well as take care of the vegetable garden. They lived in an apartment
complex where about twenty elderly Korean couples resided. Because of
his college education and some commend of English language he became
a spokesman, or head "honcho," of the Korean people living in the same
complex. He looked after them and took care of all these Korean elders'
English papers and documents which were needed to be translated into
Korean. Father and his wife was a highly respected couple who had a happy

and peaceful life. He was quite healthy without diagnosable illness and died suddenly at age 93 in January, 1995.

After my father's death, my stepmother became ill with colon cancer and was hospitalized. She told me, "Your father with the white clothes is telling me to come to him in my dream." She passed away three months later in May 1995, at the age of 83.

Photo for family gathering in 1957 after Luke left for USA. From the left back row Ik Sung, Ik Poong, Ik Nan, her husband Dr. Young Sun Kim, and Grace (prior to marriage). Front row is grandmother, father, and stepmother.

[5-4] My social activities in Seoul: I was active with the Christian student movement while I was in medical student in Seoul. At that time Mr. Sung Soo Hwang, who studied at UC Berkeley during WWII, and returned to Korea, became a lawyer and then was elected as a Korean Assemblyman and promoted to vice president of the Korean Assembly. He was a dynamic Christian leader who attracted many bright, ambitious College Christian students under the wing of his leadership.). I was the president of this organization for 2 terms

Some of the college students who were active members and made contribution to the Korean society were: Noh Jung Hyun (dean of

Management Gradaute School, Yonsei University) Cho Young Jik (CPA, LA,USA), Lee Dae Soon (Secretary of Ttransportation of the South Korea government), Oh Hee Joon (Elder), Jung Eui Young, Kim Soon Ja, Ko Jae Gun, Kim Jae Ho, Han Young Suk (Minister at the Korean Assembly of God Church in Texas), and Yoo Hyuk (professor of chemical engineering at University the of Wisconsin),Chung Byung Ho MD (surgeon in Texas), Kim Kyung Won (Korean Ambassador to the United States and Korean Ambassador to the UN), Chang Ik Tae (businessman in LA, USA).

Group meeting of the Korean Christian student fellowship under the leadership of Mr. Sung Soo Hwang (fifth from the right), author Luke (president) third from the right (Seoul, 1956).

When I was a 3rd year medical student, Mr. Park Jae Hoon, a well-known sacred music composer, and Miss Suk Jin Young, poet and publisher of a monthly magazine called Christian Ambassador and I, lived together in Suk Jin Young's house for 4 months. We said to ourselves that we were living in a convent or monastery. Our daily routine was: At 5 AM, Miss Suk would sing a hymn out loud, and then Mr. Park and I would wake up and "crawl" to her room and we did our morning prayer together. After our morning prayers, we walked outside near the small forest. While walking, Mr. Park would compose a melody in his head and returned home writing hymns into music note. He goes to church following Sunday as choir director, and then for the first time he get to played his composed hymns, because there was no piano in the Mis,Suk's home.

He's a well-known composer of some 500 hymns, most of those hymns were composed when we were living in the convent. He composed the melody for the poems written by Miss Suk Jin Young. I was the English teacher for both of them and we studied theological books in English. Later, Mr. Park became a minister and currently lives in Toronto Canada while Mr. Suk passed away 15 years ago in Los Angeles. Mr. Park composed the opera "Esther" and is currently working, almost completed opera on the theme of Yoo Kwan Soon's legendary life as a Korean Independence fighter.

[5-5] My siblings:

[5-5 A] My sister Ik Nan Kim (김익란, 金益蘭): After Ik Nan entered Sookmyung Girls High School, she became interested in drawing. She became a key member of the fine arts group at the school and was caught up with enthusiasm and inspiration from her own artwork. Ik Nan also enjoyed writing poems. Our four siblings used to sing together in beautiful quartet harmony. Those were such fond and memorable periods of my youth in spite the adverse societal conditions and our changing living circumstances.

During her high school days, Ik Nan concentrated on her painting in order to enter one of her paintings into a national art contest. She was secretly hoping that by winning the national art competition, she could convince our parents of her talent in art and persuade them to support her desire to pursue a career in Fine Arts. She was the "captain" of the Fine Arts team in her school, and she thought that she would win. But the painting of another girl in the school, Kum Soon Kim, won the contest and was accepted for the national gallery exhibition. Ik Nan was very disappointed and discouraged that her painting was rejected for the exhibit. She felt that her life had come to an end. She stayed in bed and did not go to school for two days.

Realizing how disappointed Ik Nan was, our mother told us, "If you like the fine arts so much, I guess I have to talk with your father and discuss if it is ok for you to study Fine Arts." After they discussed Ik Nan's carrier interes in fine arts They agreed and consented to her majoring in Fine Arts at college. Ik Nan then took the Ewha Women's University entrance examination and accepted into the Women's University with a major in Fine Arts.

Although Ik Nan was admitted to Ewha Women's University in 1950, when Korean War broke out, she gave up her enrollment at Ewha and worked as a bank clerk in Busan and later four and a half years as an office clerk at her alumni school Sookmyung Girls High School to help support the family, including paying my medical school tuition. I am thankful for Ik Nan's sacrifice and dedication to financially supporting the family.

Ik Nan said, "Most of my classmates were originally from Seoul, and they spoke with such a beautiful, attractive Seoul accent. My North Korean dialect was rough and sharp in contrast. They laughed at me whenever I answered the teacher's questions with my North Korean accent. I was embarrassed and became close-mouthed. Then, a classmate, Dong Yul, a girl who was born and grew up in Seoul, became my partner assigned to the same desk (usually a pair of students sat together at the same desk). She would kindly correct my accent and teach me how to speak in the standard Seoul accent. We became good friends, and we visited each other's homes after school. Because of her, I learned the Seoul accent rather quickly. I was the first one in my family to acquired the Seoul accent. After one or two years, I spoke it well and people could not believe that I came from North Korea."

There was a fellow navy recruitee, Dr. Youn Sun Kim (a graduate of Seoul National University Dental School), who entered naval basic training with me at Chinhae. He and I took a vacation after basic training and went to visit my family who were still at the Yongdo refugee camp in Busan. There he and my sister first met, began dating and finally married. My brother-in-law was discharged from the navy with the rank of Major. His father, Kim Yun Soo MD, was the first medical missionary to China from Korea.

After she had her first baby, Ik Nan entered and graduated from Seoul National University College of Fine Art majoring in western painting. Then she taught at Seunghee Girls High School for 35 years as a Fine Arts teacher and retired several years ago. She used to live near the school with her baby because her husband was on active duty with the Korean Navy.

I visited them sometimes and changed the baby's diaper. Baby Kwi-won has grown up and is now the wife of Reverend Soo Young Lee, senior pastor of Sae-moon-ahn Presbyterian Church, one of the longstanding, well established historic churches in Seoul. My sister actively engaged in painting throughout her life, and her work was accepted into the 4th, 6th, 8th, and 9th Fine Art Exhibits of the Republic of Korea. Her paintings have been displayed with such Fine Art organizations as the Association of Korean Fine Arts, the Association of Korean Women Fine Artists, as well as the Korean Christian Fine Art Association. Ik Nan's paintings have been displayed in Paris, and she has had personal exhibits twice in Seoul.

「이른 봄 날」 Oil on Canvas 60×45cm

These two paintings are by my sister Ik Nan.

「강화의 겨울」 Oil on Canvas 60.5×50cm

Luke's eightieth birthday party gathering of four siblings. From left Luke, Ik Nan, Ik Sung, Paul in May 2010 at Seal Beach Leisure World

Photo of Grace and Luke Kim at his 80th birthday Party, 2010

[5-5 B] My younger brother Ik Sung Kim

(김익성, 金益成): My younger brother Ik Sung (Ike) graduated from Seoul High School while we were refugees in Busan. He then graduated from Seoul National University College of Commerce. In 1960, he came to the United States and received an MA degree from Southern Illinois University, and went on to do PhD course work in Economics at Tulane University, New Orleans. Ik Sung finished the PhD coursework but not his thesis. Then he worked for the New York-New Jersey-Connecticut Tri-state Economic Development Commission as an economist and is now retired in New Jersey. He is a very sociable, outgoing and community minded person who served as president of the U.S. Junior Chamber of Commerce in the New York area. His wife, Soon Bong, who double majored in music (Julliard with a vocal major), and mathematics from San Jose State, worked at AT&T at the managerial level and now is retired.

[5-5 C] My youngest brother Ik Poong (Paul Kim,

김익풍,金益豊): Ik Poong (Paul), my youngest brother, graduated from Seoul High School. After high school, he became a member of the Korean Broadcasting System (KBS) Symphony Orchestra in Seoul as a flutist for two years. He then joined the Korean Army as an obligatory service for one year, and came to the United States. He studied at the University of California at Berkeley completing 5 year program for his Bachelor of Architecture. After his school, he went to New York City to work with well-known architectural firms for five years, and then came to Los Angeles where he has been practicing architecture ever since. He is one of the most productive pioneering architects in L.A. Koreatown, contributing significantly to the architectural scene and skyline. For example, he designed the popular, well-liked buildings in L.A. Koreatown such as: Oxford Palace Hotel, JJ Grand Hotel, Rotex Hotel, Ramada Hotel, and VIP Shopping Center on Olympic Blvd, which is significant because for the first time in L.A. Koreatown the genuine Korean style roof tiles were used. Paul also designed Miracle Springs Resort Hotel in Desert Hot Springs, the Zion Korean American Church of Sacramento, Reverend Kim Kae Young's memorial education and youth sanctuary building at the L.A. Youngnak Presbyterian Church, the education building of the L.A. Korean Baptist Church, and the Cerritos Presbyterian Church. Recently, he designed a skating arena, East-West Ice Palace in Artesia, for five time World Figure Skating champion Michelle Kwan. Currently Korean figure skating heroine Yuna Kim practices here at East-West Ice Palace with Michelle Kwan. Globally, he worked on master plan for Amador Islands in Panama and International School in Ulaanbaatar in Mongolia. Most recently, he designed the AR Galleria Shopping Mall in Garden Gove, Ca.

Lobby at Oxford Palace Hotel, Koreatown Los Angeles,1992.

Oxford Palace Hotel, LA

East-west Ice Palace, Artesia, CA. (Michelle Kwan's Skating Arena and Kim Yun Ah practice also)

A R Galleria Shopping Center Garden Grove, 2008.

J. J. Grand Hotel, Koreatown Los Angeles

Zion Presbyterrian Church, Sacrameto, California, 2009

Chapter 6.

My Life in the US as a Graduate Student, Married Man and a First Generation Immigrant Asian American Psychiatrist (1956 to present)

[6-1] Going to the U.S. with two hundred dollars in my pocket: After the Korean War ended, most buildings and houses were destroyed and the economic condition was so poor that the Gross National Product (GNP) of Korea was only 96 dollars per person. In the midst of those adverse conditions, I was notified by the Korean government that, after three days of vigorous examination given by the Ministry of Foreign Affairs, I was selected for sponsorship/scholarship by the U.S. Air Force Officers Wives Association. Having an American sponsor was required to enter the United States with a student visa and I had already accepted a medicine internship in Tucson, Arizona, so everything was in place. The U.S. Air Force Officers Wives Association sponsorship was not a traditional scholarship because there was no promise of financial assistance.

I crossed the Pacific Ocean by ship because it was before the beginning of transpacific flight travel. In June, 1956, I left Busan harbor on a Korean merchant marine cargo ship. There were six students aboard who had agreed to work a few hours each day on the ship in order to pay a $200 passage fare, saving $150 from the regular passenger ship rate. We learned from each other later that those of us not used to the western toilet system were unnecessarily squatting on the top of the toilet seat! On the way, the ship stopped at Osaka for one day and we got off to do some sightseeing in the city. I remember that we bought an umbrella for one dollar.

For some unknown reason, the ship went to a small fishing village in Oregon called Newport. It took three days for the immigration officers to come onboard to process us because the ship was anchored several miles away from shore.

After going through the immigration process, we were authorized to get off the ship and took a Greyhound bus to Berkeley, California. We met some members of the U.S. Air Force Officers Wives Association in Berkeley and we checked into the YMCA for two nights because we were told that at five dollars a night it was the cheapest place to stay. From Berkeley, I went to Los Angeles to see a Korean friend of mine, Yu Hyuk, a fellow scholarship recipient who came several months earlier. Mr. Yu later became a well-known professor of organic chemistry at the University of Wisconsin. From Los Angeles to Tucson, Arizona I again took a Greyhound bus. It was very long tiring bus ride and I was exhausted by the time I arrived in Tucson. I was surprised and somewhat disappointed to see the desert flatland of Arizona because my image of America had been one full of trees, mountains, and scenery which I had seen on movies.

[6-2] Rotating Medical Internship and Graduate Study in Clinical Psychology at University of Arizona: Before coming to the U.S. I applied for a rotating medical internship position being offered by several hospitals scattered across the United States. I received a nice letter from St. Mary's Hospital and Pima County Hospital in Tucson, Arizona saying that I was accepted for their medical internship in their hospitals. It was my first acceptance letter so I decided to go to Arizona. I had no idea what kind of place Tucson was. I looked at a map and pronounced the placement as "Tuck-son," not knowing that the "c" was silent. In June 1956, I started my internship at St. Mary's Hospital and my first 3 month assignment was to the OB-GYN department where I delivered about 100 babies including two breach

deliveries of two sets of twins without any difficulty on problems. In June 1957, I completed one year of my rotating medical internship at St. Mary's Hospital and Pima County Hospital where I treated many Native American and Mexican American patients.

Luke Kim's living quarters for interns. Daytime study in the university and working at the emergency room at night

[6-3] Colloquial English: Although I was relatively fluent in English, I encountered some comical and yet embarrassing situations during my hospital work because I did not know simple slang or colloquial English.

For example, a food server at the hospital cafeteria corrected me when I asked for "*Smashed* potatoes please." She asked me, "Do you mean 'mashed potatoes?'" With embarrassment I responded, "Yes, mashed potatoes please."

While I was assisting a surgeon in the operation room, the surgeon told me to "let it go" while I was holding onto a suture thread which he was working with. I asked him "Go where?" literally interpreting "let it *go*". He shouted at me "Let it *go*!" An operation room nurse nearby said "'Let it go' means 'release the thread.'"

A Native Indian patient came to the hospital emergency room. He replied repeatedly "Damned if I knew! . . ." "Damned if I knew! . . ." to my questions, regardless what question I asked. I had a hard time particularly understanding his pronunciation with his squeaky, high pitched voice "Damned if I knew . . . damned if I knew." I had never heard before such an expression in my life. So I had to get help from an ER nurse.

The first thing I did after I received my first $100 monthly internship stipend was to buy a blue colored stone brooch and mail it to Kyung Ja (Grace.) I mailed it to her because while on a date one evening Grace and I were at a department store in Seoul and found a beautiful blue colored brooch that I wanted to buy for her but I did not have enough money in my pockets. I was very embarrassed about the situation. Grace says she no longer has the brooch because in 1962 when she left for the United States, she gave it to her sister. Years later, Grace's sister Kay gave a beautiful blue colored stone pendant to Grace as a birthday gift.

Several months later, I bought a flute on a monthly installment basis, and sent it to Ik Poong (Paul). At that time, Paul was a very good flute player. However, he did not have his own flute but used a flute belonging to Seoul High School. He became so good with the new flute Luke bought for him that he became a flutist with KBS symphony Orchestra, a premier professional orchestra in Korea for 2 years before coming to the U.S.A.

After completing my 12 month medical internship, I enrolled at the University of Arizona in September, 1957 where I undertook a PhD course in clinical psychology. In order to be able to attend university classes during the day, I worked at the Pima County Hospital emergency room at night. As compensation, I was able to live in the interns quarters and with this arrangement my room and board were taken care of. I completed and received my PhD in Clinical Psychology in July 1960. My dissertation was entitled, "A Study of Bender-Gestalt Tests with Different Clinical Groups."

From Arizona I went to Buffalo, New York where I did a one year internship in clinical psychology. I continued on to complete my psychiatric residency program at the Buffalo State Hospital and the University of Buffalo Medical School.

PhD degree in Clinical Psychology awarded at the University of Arizona in 1960

[6-4] Six-year separation from Grace and one telephone call: Grace and I exchanged letters once a week during

our six year separation. I am regretful that we no longer have those love letters in our possession. Somehow they were misplaced or lost during moving. Through this period of letter writing, we came to know each other at a much deeper level.

Until the 1970s, very few Korean households had a private telephone at home. In order to call Grace over the phone, I had to make an arrangement with the International Telephone company beforehand so that she would be at the phone company office at a pre-arranged time. We did this only once over the six years. Grace had to go to the Seoul office of the international telephone company and waited for my telephone call at the exact pre-arranged time. I called, she answered, however when we started speaking over the phone, Grace was surprised and started laughing at my Korean which she said sounded like an American missionary speaking Korean. In those days there were very few Korean students on the University of Arizona campus so I had very little opportunity to speak Korean. So she laughed and laughed and could not speak. The three minutes passed by so fast and that was our only telephone conversation over those years.

Years later when Grace was teaching at the Davis Senior High School in Davis she told her students about our six years of letter writing and they responded, "You mean six weeks or six months?" Grace said, "No, six years." They were dumbfounded saying, "It's impossible not to see each other for six years and still continue the relationship."

[6-5] Grace's encounter with orphaned teenagers:

Grace graduated from the Teachers College of Seoul National University (SNU) in 1956, the same year that I graduated from SNU Medical School. Right after graduation she began to teach at Seunghee Girls High School as a regular teacher. This is the same school where my sister Ik Nan later taught Fine Arts.

One day she saw gangsters fighting near the Yongsan station. She approached to stop the fighting. One of the teenage gang members saw Grace and said, "You were my teacher when I was at Cheju Orphanage." Grace did not recognize him because when she had known him he was five or six years old, but now he was a teenager. The teenager said that after they left the orphanage, they roamed around and came to the Yongsan railroad station area in Seoul where they slept on the street. They survived by pick-pocketing near the railroad station. Grace asked him, "What's your dream? What would you like to do to fulfill your dreams?" He told Grace that his dream was to be a high school student with a school uniform and school badge and he wanted to complete his studies.

So Grace took several orphaned teenagers home and fed them. Then she consulted with her father about what these orphaned teenagers wanted to do. Her father said, "We have to do something about these teenagers and give them the opportunity to study in high school." Grace started planning for an evening vocational school. Together with the Yongsan Police Chief and National Assemblyman Hwang Sung Soo, she went around factories nearby Yongsan and asked the company heads to give these orphaned teenagers jobs and a place to stay. Then she solicited her colleagues and friends who were teaching in regular high schools to volunteer to teach these orphaned teenagers in the evening without pay. About 20 teachers volunteered to teach in the evening.

The police chief was happy to help with Grace's plan because it would solve his problems dealing with the teenagers who were committing crimes in the neighborhood. Assemblymen Hwang was a leader of a Christian student movement at that time and was impressed by Grace's enthusiastic plans and visions for those teenage orphans, so he arranged for buildings to be used for evening classes and furthermore negotiated with the government to provide land to build permanent school buildings. The Korean American Foundation helped to secure textbooks and school supplies. The U.S. Air Force expressed interest in helping to build the permanent school facility on government land.

Grace and her volunteer friends were excited about this plan and vision for a vocational school. They submitted the plan to the government, and the Ministry of Education not only approved the proposal, but also appointed Grace to be the Principal of "Yongsan Vocational High School." She was only 26 years old at the time.

Then, suddenly, the 4.19 students uprising happened and resulted in the demise of Syngman Rhee's presidency and the Liberal Party of which Assemblyman Hwang was a member. Grace's plan and vision for the vocational school came to a halt, leaving her in financial debt for the completed architectural drawings and blueprints for new school buildings.

Congratulatory Remarks
Grace Kim's main supporter Mr. Sung Soo Hwang, national assembly man.

Students of Young San vocational evening school.

Grace, Principal of the Young San vocational evening school
for orphan teenagers.

Volunteer teachers meet after class at Young San vocational night
school for orphan.

‘小花，공부를 맞치고 ‥‥‥
— 4283. 10. 9 —

Teachers meet with the co-ed students after school.

School ID card. The magazine article about Grace's dedicated work as a
Principal for the teenage orphans.

[6-6] Our Wedding in Buffalo, New York: I completed all the necessary training in preparation for my return to Korea with the plan to develop a new PhD course in Clinical Psychology at SNU Medical School. This plan had been discussed and mutually agreed upon between Professor Nam Myungsuk, chairman of the SNU Psychiatry Department, and myself before I left Korea. Unfortunately the plan did not workout because of the untimely death of Professor Nam. I decided to remain in the United States and asked Grace if she could come to America to marry me. She said yes.

Luke and Grace Wedding, Buffalo, N.Y. 1962.

Wedding for Luke and Grace without parents of both sides present.
about 100 friends came from the church, hospital and few Korean friends.

Newlywed couple at Niagara Fall in 1962.

Honeymoon picture at Empire State Building in New York.

[6-7] Ms. Jeannette Thompson as our "Godmother": Following Grace's arrival in April, 1962, there was a one month waiting period for our wedding. Ms. Jeanette Thompson took Grace under her wing and was happy to help her prepare for the wedding. Ms. Thompson planned and organized our wedding, including soliciting her church women's organization to prepare the wedding reception with a wedding cake, drinks and food. One month later we got married at Bethany Presbyterian Church in Buffalo. It was a small wedding, without parents or relatives of either side, but with a few Korean and hospital friends. Although I was a Psychiatric Resident who was relatively poor financially, it was the most exciting and happiest time in my life.

Ms. Thompson was my landlord from whom I rented a room while I was doing my psychiatric residency at Buffalo State Hospital. She was an 82 year old widow who lost her only son in a WWII Pacific Island battle. She treated me like her own son. In the same way, Ms. Thompson treated Grace as her own daughter and taught her many tasks necessary for the American life. For example, she taught Grace how to use coupons in grocery shopping, how to clean house using a vacuum cleaner, how to make simple clothes using patterns, and finally how to cook holiday meals for Thanksgiving, Easter, and Christmas. Grace was most grateful to Ms. Thompson who gave to her a wonderful orientation of the American way of life. Both of us feel that Ms. Thompson had been, more or less, our "Godmother."

After the wedding, we went to New York for our honeymoon. We took a picture at the Empire State Building (see the photo). Originally, we planned to stay in New York for a week and we met my brother, Ik Sung, there. He had finished his master's degree at Southern Illinois University and was working at a resort hotel near New York City during summer vacation. He was a doctoral student in Economics at Tulane University, New Orleans. Ik Sung was working very hard as a hotel busboy to make money to move on to Tulane University. I felt sorry for his financial struggles. Grace and I decided to cut short our New York visit and gave him the rest of the leftover money.

Newlywed wife Grace, washing dishes

[6-8] Driving my 59 Chevy from Buffalo to Vacaville, California across the country: We decided to

settle in Northern California. However, until we actually moved to CA, I did not realize how difficult it was in the 1960s for foreign medical graduates (FMGs) to apply for a California Medical License. The California Medical Board did not allow licensing based on reciprocity with other U.S. states. The California Medical Board emphasized that there were no exceptions.

Someone facetiously said that even if Sigmund Freud were to apply for a California Medical License as a FMG, he would have to go through the same process, including an additional one year of internship in California. I understand that following the passage of the 1960's immigration reform bill, the requirements for FMG's securing a medical license have been liberalized considerably, including allowing for state-to-state reciprocity. But the immigration reform bill had not yet passed and until I received my medical license, I was qualified for and worked as a clinical psychologist.

Grace and I drove across the country from Buffalo to California in my 1959 Chevrolet carrying all the stuff that we possessed, wedding gifts received, and some books. At that time, Grace was six months pregnant with our first son, David. Our doctor advised us to be safe and not to drive more than 300 miles a day. It was a cold February with snow blizzards. On the highway near Chicago, our car skidded on the slippery highway and got stuck in a snow bank. We waited several hours before a tow truck came to rescue us. Finally, we reached Sacramento. We were surprised and happy to see pretty flowers and green scenery after driving through the Eastern part of the United States which was barren, gray in color and covered with snow. Fortunately there was no serious medical problem with Grace's pregnancy.

Grace in front of 59 Chevy which we drove across country from
New York to California

[6-9] Another medical internship in California:

After I passed basic science examination, i.e. anatomy, physiology, organic chemistry, etc. I did my additional year in a rotating internship at Mt. Zion Hospital in San Francisco. And then I passed Clinical examination and finally received my California Medical license. Surprisingly to my unexpected benefit, I spent the first six months in the neurosurgical operating room and there worked mostly with UCSF Professor of Neurosurgery Dr. Bertram Feinstein. He is the late husband of U.S. Senator Dianne Feinstein. While assigned to the Department of Internal Medicine for the second six months of clinical rotation, I was lucky enough to spend a substantial amount of time at the famous San Francisco Psychoanalytic Institute, located next to Mt. Zion Hospital. There, I had the privilege of attending great lectures and workshops given by well known faculty members and guest lecturers, such as Erik Erikson, Robert Wallerstein, Joseph Weiss, George Sampson, Mardi Horowitz and others.

Eventually, I grew a little bored with orthodox Freudian theory and began searching for more "liberal" and flexible schools of psychotherapy. At that time, San Francisco was a Mecca for all kinds of new trendsetting ideas and it was the peak of the Hippie Movement in the Haight-Ashbury district where I used to visit. There I was exposed to, and attended, workshops on Gestalt Therapy (with Fritz Pearl), Transactional Analysis, Rolfing, and Psychosynthesis.

In subsequent years, I have become more interested in spirituality, meditation/prayer, and Transpersonal Psychotherapy. I am interested in and have attempted the integration of Eastern and Western philosophies and religions. As a result, I have become more "eclectic and flexible in my psychotherapeutic approach with Korean/Asian American patients. As I get older, I have been even more interested in spirituality and psychotherapy. With Dr. Seung Duck Cheung, MD, a former professor of psychiatry at Youngnam University School of Medicine, we published a Korean translation of Seymour Boorstein's "Transpersonal Psychotherapy," as well as two other related books in Korean.

While interning in San Francisco I composed the song "yearning for my home beyond the golden gate bridge". Words and music are my work. I was home sick and melancholic. I was expressing my feelings through the music.

Yearning for My Home Beyond Golden Gate Bridge
by Luke Kim (words & music)

Sunset over the Golden Gate Bridge;
Romantic fog over the bridge.

I am longing for the memories of my sweet home town
Beyond the Pacific Ocean.

I am yearning for home.

After a hard day of work,
I am on my way home.
My family is waiting for me...

My happy moment is to gaze at the smiling faces
of my wife and children.

My thankful moment is to see
the peaceful faces of my family members.

I am hurrying ...
hurrying on my way home.

Wood carving art work by Luke Kim

[6-10] My Prison Psychiatrist Days at Vacaville

Medical Facility: In 1970, I became Chief of Research and Staff Development at the California Medical Facility (CMF) of the California Department of Corrections, located in Vacaville. At that time, California Medical Facility was the premier psychiatric treatment and rehabilitation center within the national forensic field, attracting students, scholars and professional visitors from all over the world for field trips, training, study and research.

While at Vacaville, I developed and directed the California Department of Corrections' very successful career psychiatric residency program in conjunction with Napa State Hospital of the California Department of Mental Health.

While chief psychiatrist there, I evaluated and provided therapy and treatment with rather "infamous" inmates such as Charles Manson the mass murderer of actress Sharon Tate and others, Sirhan Sirhan who shot and killed Senator Robert Kennedy during his presidential campaign, and Juan Corona, a mass murderer who killed and buried more than 30 farm workers. Timothy Leary, an ex-Harvard psychology professor and LSD guru, was also in our prison on drug charges. I hired him as one of my prison inmate research assistants for three years. He talked quite a bit about the outer space planetary world where we could eventually live. He was ahead of his time.

The star sign in the chest is Luke Kim
Staffs at the Vacaville Medical Facility

[6-11] Contributions to the psychiatric profession and UC Davis:

I coordinated joint research projects at CMF-Vacaville with the University of California Davis (UCD) Medical School's Department of Psychiatry where I had been a clinical faculty member. This research was in addition to my seminar series on clinical psychology and forensic clinical issues presented at the UCD Medical Center in Sacramento. In 1973, with Dr. Joe Tupin, then UCD professor and Chair of the Psychiatry Department, and other faculty members, I conducted the early pioneering study on the use of Lithium Carbonate in the treatment of violent psychopathic bipolar prisoners with a very positive outcome. After the study, one subject complained, "I have lost my identity now because I lost my feelings of rage and anger."

Another area of my interest has been the mental health of immigrants, especially Korean Americans and Asian Americans. I wrote a chapter titled, "Psychiatric Care of Korean Americans" in *Culture, Ethnicity and Mental Illness* edited by Albert Gaw (American Psychiatric Press, 1993). That book has become a standard textbook in cultural psychiatry. In my chapter, I touched briefly on the topic of "Korean Ethos" (culture-philosophy) which I expanded on further in a paper that I presented at the Annual Conference of the Academy of Psychoanalysis and Psychotherapy in 1994. I believe this was the first time the concept of "Korean Ethos" was presented to mainstream psychiatrists assembled at a national psychiatric gathering.

From left, professor and chair of the psychiatry, Robert Hales M.D., Russell Lim M.D., Chair of the diversity advisory committee, Allen Korike M.D professor of psychiatry, Luke Kim M.D., and Claire Pomeroy, M.D. M.B.A, Dean of UC Davis Medical School.

[6-12] Introducing Korean Ethos: Here I would like to introduce briefly the concepts of Korean Ethos. In order to better understand Korean people, it is helpful to know something about the ethos influencing Korean psyche, social attitudes and behavior. Korean Ethos includes *Jeong* (정,情), *Haan* (한,恨), *O-gi* (오기, 傲氣), *che-myun*(체면,體面), *Nonchi* (눈치), *Palja* (八字), and *Muht* (멋).

(For further discussion in detail please refer to the full text of a journal article in the Appendix 6)

Jeong: *Jeong* is an emotive (sensitive) Korean term referring to a special interpersonal bonding, trust and emotional closeness; *Jeong* is an important word within Korean ethos. There is no English equivalent for *jeong*. It encompasses the meanings of a wide range of English terms—emotional attachment and bonding, empathy, affinity, we-feeling, and love.

Jeong strengthens the bonding of relationships between friends, teachers and students, or parents and children. *Jeong* is considered an essential element in human life, promoting the depth and richness of personal relations. With *jeong,* relationships are made deeper and longer lasting. In times of social upheaval, calamity, and unrest, *jeong* is the only binding and stabilizing force in human relationships. Without *jeong,* life would be emotionally barren, and a person would feel isolated and disconnected from others. *Jeong* brings about the "special" feelings in relationships: togetherness, sharing, bonding, and "we-feeling (*woo-ri*)." *Jeong* is what makes us say "we" rather than "I," and "ours" instead of "mine."

The concept of love has been richly dealt with in the history of Western culture and religions. The Western concept of love includes a variety of types: divine love (Agape), erotic love, maternal love, brotherly/sisterly love, platonic love, altruistic love to name a few. But *jeong* does not fit into any one of these categories. *Jeong* is the common denominator within all of these types of love. "Love" is a beautiful and power ful English word, but unfortunately the word has been overused, commercialized, and sexualized to the degree that the word "love" had lost its clarity, beauty and meaning. *Jeong* can be love in the Western sense, but there are important differences in the nuance and quality. I would characterize those differences as follows:

LOVE (Western)

-   more direct in expression

- more physical, behavioral
- more action-oriented
- active, positive, forward, outward
- more need/desire-related
- more intentional, volitional
- tends to be possessive
- more contractual
- differentiated with boundary—separated self
- happiness, joy

JEONG (Asian)

- more indirect in emotional expression
- more affective, attitudinal
- more relational
- more inward, yearning for, waiting and thinking of
- more survival—and connection-related
- more naturally developing
- not fall in love at first sight, but requires an incubation period to develop bonding
- could be passive/aggressive
- tends to be protective
- more unconditional
- enduring warmth, care and love
- less differentiated, and more fused
- more "good earth-mother" archetype

In contrast to the western concept of love, the imagery of *jeong* is quiet, gentle, nurturing, caring, giving, trusting, loyal, considerate, devoted, dependable, and sacrificial.

Reflecting on the above list of adjectives, I feel that the *jeong* concept has a more feminine quality of love, similar to the "self-in-relation" theory of the feminine psychology which emphasizes caring, connectedness and nurturing relations in love.

Haan: *Haan* refers to feelings of anger, resentment, or a grudge. It is a form of a victimization syndrome in which *haan*-ridden Koreans feel victimized or unjustly treated. Some Korean psychiatrists think that *haan* is deeply imprinted in the collected subconscious of Koreans, who have endured much in their history. They make the analogy of the Jewish psyche and its connection to the Holocaust. *Haan* is an important and dynamic contributing factor to the manifestation of mixed clinical features of depression, anxiety, and somatization, which is called *hwa-byung*, a traditional Korean folk medical term.

O-gi: *O-gi* is based on *haan*-related emotions, such as anger, victimization, and failure/defeat in the past. *O-gi* is an intense and concentrated desire and effort to conquer, surpass, and win over the rivals who had victimized or gave him or her strong *haan*—related emotions and given experiences. For example, the one who failed the business or college entrance examination in the past may double the efforts to succeed the second time.

Che-myun: *Che-myun* means "face-saving." As in other Asian countries, face-saving behavior is very important to Koreans in their public and social relationships. Maintaining *che-myun* protects the dignity and self-respect of the individual as well as of his or her family. Honor is considered an important concept to live by for Koreans and the honor is maintained by *che-myun*. *Che-myun* helps to promote harmonious relationships. For example, face-saving may help a person to behave more gracefully and peacefully. *Che-myun* helps to moderate his or her temper, even if the person is angry with the individual he/she is facing directly. *Che-myun* also promotes the development of mutual responsibilities and obligations, because a person loses face if he or she does not respond in a reciprocal manner. *Che-myun* is conducive to the development of a reciprocal bond and relationship between and among people.

Noonchi: In Western culture, verbal communication, explicitly and clearly expressed, is the main mode of communication. However, in Asian culture, communication is often subtle, indirect, and nonverbal. In Korean, *noonchi* means "measuring with eyes." It is an intuitive, sixth-sense perception of another person—a capacity for sizing up and evaluating another person through heightened awareness of and sensitivity to the person's gestures, facial expressions, and other nonverbal cues.

Palja: *Palja* means fate and destiny and is derived from the terminology of fortune telling. In traditional Korean society, a person's role and life status have been essentially predetermined, and people have little control over their lives. How, then, do they cope with the woes of life and their misfortunes? They accept their *palja* with a stoic, fatalistic attitude.

Perhaps that is why religions such as Buddhism and Taoism are appealing to some Koreans because they help them accept *palja* more readily.

Muht: *Muht* is a Korean word meaning exquisite, beautiful, splendid, and elegant. A person of *muht* is someone who knows how to enjoy life and can appreciate nature, art, music, and poetry. The ethos of *muht*: probably promotes the development of exquisite musical, artistic, and other cultural tastes and appreciation among Koreans.

My article on Korean Ethos has been popularized, quoted, and frequently referred to in newspaper and magazine articles over the years. In addition, I have authored four chapters, three books and numerous articles in journals and magazines.

[6-13] Contributions to the American Psychiatric Association (APA) and Association of Korean American Psychiatrists (AKAP): In the early 1970s, the American Psychiatric Association (APA) president appointed me as one of three charter members of the new APA Taskforce on Asian American Psychiatrists (AAP). The Taskforce ultimately made recommendations to the APA president to establish the Committee of Asian American Psychiatrists within APA structure. Subsequently, I served the AAP committee as a member for six years as well as serving as the editor-in-chief of the committee's newsletter for five years.

In 1979, I organized and founded a grassroots professional organization called Association of Korean American Psychiatrists Association (AKAP) and served as its first president for two years. My call for action took place during the annual APA convention in Chicago and 31 APA member Korean American psychiatrists met to formally establish AKAP. (see my AKAP 1995s report as founding present below).

At the 1997 American Psychiatric Association's (APA) annual convention held in San Diego, I was honored to receive the APA's highly coveted Dr. Kun Po Soo Asian American Award, which is given to one individual each year for "making significant contributions toward understanding the impact and import of Asian cultural heritage in areas relevant to psychiatry."

At the 2002 APA convention in San Francisco, I presented the paper in which I shared my experiences and observations in running a small community mental health in Galt, California. (For the detail, please see the article, "Therapeutic approach of the Jeong-based relationship", appendix number seven). There I applied the concept and philosophy of *Jeong* in developing the interpersonal relationships among clinic staff. The resulting family-like atmosphere through jeong-rich bonding and emotional closeness with emphasis of mutual reciprocity afforded this clinic some unique advantages in personnel management in contrast to pure business-like and efficiency-oriented clinics.

ASSOCIATION OF KOREAN AMERICAN PSYCHIATRISTS (AKAP)

January 1995 Report
Luke I.C. Kim, M.D. Ph.D.
Founding President, AKAP

Historical background of AKAP:

Few Korean physicians came to the United States for postgraduate training prior to the Korean War. Beginning in the mid-1950's, however, a gradual but steady stream of Korean physicians left Korea for intern and/or residency training in the US.

Koreans experienced great tragedy and pain during the Korean War and post-war economic hardship. Therefore, it is not surprising that a significant number of Korean physicians in the U.S. in the early days were attracted to psychiatry. This is because many of them became interested in human problems and human nature. In addition, state hospitals tended to offer more generous stipends for psychiatric residents compared to other specialties. And there were plenty of psychiatric resident positions available.

Unfortunately, a two-tiered system of psychiatry developed in the United States: private practice psychiatry and public psychiatry. The majority of US graduate American psychiatrists, more or less, ignored the large segment of the severely and/or chronically mentally ill population who were being cared for in state hospitals and public mental health clinics. Many American psychiatrists were mainly interested in setting up plush private practices in fashionable locations, such as Beverly Hills, Boston or New York, doing psychotherapy with "neurotic" young, attractive, articulate, "psychologically minded clients.

That's why state hospitals were desperate in recruiting psychiatrists. IMG (International Medical Graduates) physicians have filled the void and have become the backbone of the psychiatric staff in American public psychiatry. Moreover, during the period of the 1950s and early 60's, it was almost impossible for IMGs to get into top—notch university psychiatric residency programs. University doors started to open up for IMGs only after immigration laws were liberalized in 1965 as well as the advent of affirmative action. As a result, some Korean psychiatrists received excellent psychiatric residency training in university settings. After the mid-1980s, however, the federal government and AMA began to close the doors again on IMGs for intern and residency training programs.

IMGs currently represent one third of the total membership of the American Psychiatric Association. Moreover, many IMGs did not join APA because they felt that APA was geared toward the private practice model of American psychiatrists at the expense of the needs of IMG's and public psychiatry.

In 1975, then APA president appointed a three-member Ad Hoc Committee (Linddy Sata, MD of Seattle WA; Betty Chan, MD of Boston MA; Luke Kim, MD of Davis CA) to address the professional needs of Asian American psychiatrists, and to recommend how the APA can encourage Asian American psychiatrists to actively participate in APA functions and activities. After extensive caucus meetings and deliberation, the committee recommended that the APA establish a standing committee of Asian American Psychiatrists within the APA. The APA implemented this recommendation in 1976. Since that time, the 6 member committee of Asian American psychiatrists has made significant contributions to addressing the needs of Asian American psychiatrists_ The Korean members of the committee at the present time are: Dr. Wun Jung Kim (vice-chair) and Dr. Chang Hee Lee.

The APA Asian American Caucus also encouraged the formation of grass-roots ethnic psychiatric organizations. The Association of Korean American Psychiatrists (AKAP) was officially established in 1979 in Chicago during the annual scientific convention of the American Psychiatric Association. AKAP has been active in its advocacy role and has become more politically visible within the APA. According to 1991 data from the APA, there were 315 APA members with Korean surnames. We know that also there are at least 200—250 unaccounted for, non-APA member Korean psychiatrists in the U.S.

Other Asian Pacific psychiatric organizations, larger than AKAP in membership, are Indian and Pakistan Psychiatric Associations (1,000 + members), and Filipino American psychiatrists group (600+ APA members).

AKAP Activities:

In the first ten years, the AKAP was mainly a social organization which held an annual dinner party during the APA annual meetings. However, in the last several years, AKAP has become much more active and substantial in its operation and programs. During or in tandem with the APA annual convention, AKAP has held annual banquet dinners and business meetings, as well as a half-day to one-day AKAP symposium on topics that are culturally relevant to Korean! Asian American populations. AKAP also has regional activities. KA psychiatrists in California, for example, has held a yearly scientific meeting of the AKAP California District Society in Los Angeles (once in Las Vegas). Mental health professionals of multiple disciplines have been invited to the meetings. The AKAP California District Society has been able to develop professional networking and mutual referral systems with allied mental health workers, such as clinical psychologists, psychiatric social workers, marriage/family/child counselors, substance abuse counselors, Korean owners/operators of board and care, senior day care center, schools for Korean immigrants' drunken drivers, shelter for Korean battered women, etc.

AKAP's president is elected annually. The current and 17th president of AKAP is Dr. Christopher Chung (SNU,72), Director of Psychiatric Emergency Services at UCLA-Harbor Medical Center. President-elect is Dr.Won Il Choi (SNU,70), chief psychiatrist of a large health care organization, MCC, in Los Angeles.

Dr. Chol Lee (Y onsei, 61), the current president of the Korean American Medical Association, was the 3rd president of the AKAP. More recent presidents include: David Rue (Texas U,), Director of child and adolescent services, Cleveland Clinic; Dr. Chang Hee Lee (Korea, 70), Director of Lee Psychiatric Group, Inc., Los Angeles; Dr. Tai Pyung Yoo (Chunnam,59), CEO of Henry Ford Mercy Health Network; Dr. Wun Jung Kim (SNU,75), Associate Professor of Child Psychiatry, Medical College of Ohio.

AKAP has been publishing its newsletter three or four times a year. A membership directory was published and has been revised since. During the Los Angeles riots, KA psychiatrists in the LA area offered dedicated voluntary services to the victims of Korean immigrants in Koreatown.

Also AKAP members made scientific presentations on the LA Riots and psychiatric findings of the Korea town victims at the APA annual convention. Also Chun-Kee Ryu M.D. presented data on the types and characteristics of the psychiatric patients seen at his private practice office.

In the past few years, there has been an active exchange of ideas through joint meetings between AKAP members and psychiatrists in Korea, China, Japan and even Russia. AKAP members have actively participated in the scientific programs of the Pacific Rim College of Psychiatrists.

Since 1990, AKAP has been offering a traveling scholarship to a psychiatric resident in Korea who is screened and selected by the Korean Neuropsychiatric Association for the best research paper. Through the scholarship, the resident is invited to attend the APA annual scientific convention, as well as present his or her research paper at the AKAP symposium.

Beginning in 1995, in a reciprocal manner, the Korean Neuropsychiatric Association has offered a traveling scholarship to a Korean American psychiatric resident who is screened and selected by AKAP as the best KA psychiatric resident based on his/her research interest and commitment to KA community.

The membership of AKAP has remained constant over the last 10 years with no replenishment of new doctors from Korea except for a small number of 1.5 or 2nd generation KA physicians who have specialized in psychiatry. It is anticipated that membership will decrease through retirement or death of current members. Therefore, it is essential for AKAP to promote psychiatry as a career for young Korean American medical students, and to recruit and groom a new generation of KA psychiatrists.

Finally, for the interest of readers, the following are examples of the subject matters presented and discussed at AKAP symposiums.

1991:—Korean ethos: concepts of Jeong and Haan
    —Uprooting and rerooting: adjustment and mental health stages of Korean immigrants in the USA
    —Family therapy with Korean Americans
    —Our children: our future: Round Table discussion

1992—Transcultural adoption of Asian Children
—Korean American Patients in psychiatric emergency services.
—Transcultural psychopharmacology
—Korean American psychiatrists as a psychiatric administrator

1993—Concept of the Self East Asian mind
—Psychiatry and Confucian teachings
—Los Angeles Riots Korean victims
—Clinical perspective
—Anthropological perspective

1994—Substance abuse in the Korean American community of the New York area
—Cross cultural aspects of mental health and illness of Korean elderly immigrants
—Inter-racial, inter-ethnic marriage of KA population:
—Sociology and dynamics interracial marriage
—Genetics of inter-ethnic marriage
—Panel discussion by interracially married couples of KA psychiatrist

[6-14] Cultural Psychiatry: I have been promoting cultural psychiatry in an effort to emphasize a better understanding of the cultural differences as well as similarities between the East and West. Psychiatric diagnosis and treatment methods and outcomes of the mainly Caucasian population have been well documented; it is not so with minority populations, especially Asian Americans. For example, when treating depression, western-oriented diagnosis and treatment approaches for Asian American patients have limited success partly due to language and culture differences. In cultural psychiatry, I feel that it is important to study and be familiar with the patient's traditional culture, customs, value system, thought processes, and communication style which are all helpful in developing an effective diagnosis and treatment of psychiatric disorders.

For example, a depressed Korean American patient sees a Caucasian psychiatrist for the first time for a consultation and initial evaluation for diagnosis.

If the Caucasian psychiatrist asks the patient:

"Do you feel depressed?" or "Do you feel sad?" or "Do you feel like you wanted to die?"

The Korean patient may likely reply "no" to these questions.

However, if the Caucasian psychiatrist who is familiar with cultural psychiatry may ask the same patient:

"Do you have experience of *haan* that has bothered you in your life?" The patient is more likely to reply "yes" and then elaborate on *haan* feelings that the patient has experienced in life. This opens up the conversation and information is more readily and freely provided. Subsequent conversation becomes more meaningful and richer. This kind of conversation leads to more accurate diagnoses and effective treatment approaches because the patient knows that the Caucasian psychiatrist is familiar with Korean people's emotions and psyche and therefore, she/ he may feel more comfortable continuing with the doctor.

[6-15] Our Lives Dedicated to Community Service: Grace comes from a background of community service. Public service is as much a part of her life as it is of mine.

During her college years, Grace used to go to the rural areas during her summer vacations where she would gather children from poor and disadvantaged families. She planned group activities under what she calls "education toward enlightenment." It was as if she were a Peace Corps or missionary teacher in a disadvantaged country. She likened our community service commitment to that of Peace Corps workers because the Peace Corps serves to "educate toward enlightenment" the disadvantaged and less educated. Grace also worked at a Cheju Island orphanage during the Korean War for two years. Her experience in working with orphans inspired and influenced her to choose the Child and Human Development major for her graduate study, as well as her continuing interest in the welfare of orphans and adoptees.

We feel that this kind of life philosophy and orientation continued throughout our married life, and that our life purpose, lifestyle, and value orientations have not changed much in those 40 years. The central theme of our service to community has been "education toward enlightenment," whether it is through the roles we play as a community organizer, community leader, teacher or mentor.

[6-16] Supporting "worthy causes of Education Toward Enlightenment": Grace and I have lived on salaried incomes, and are now on fixed limited retirement pensions. Nonetheless, it

has been and continues to be our practice to contribute financial support to worthy causes whenever an opportunity arises.

Our favorite causes were those that provided leadership development and scholarships for Korean American/Asian American young people. We have supported the programs of community organizations such as the Korean American Coalition (KAC), Council of Asian Pacific Islanders together for advocacy and leadership (CAPITAL), Korean American Adoptee and Adoptive Family Network (KAAN), among others. For example, we contributed $10,000 a year for five years to KAC. Grace and I had been board members or advisors of these organizations for many years.

I would like to highlight five programs that we have supported through the mechanism of endowment funding. The advantage of endowment funding is that our contribution provides financial support permanently year after year to the target project because the funding released is derived from the interest or dividends of the deposited endowment fund contribution.

Our endowment funding contributions have been to:

1) Travel expense scholarships given each year to two psychiatric residents competitively selected from the U.S. Psychiatric residency programs and Korean Psychiatric residency programs. Each recipient presents his/her research paper at either the annual scientific conference of the Association of Korean American Psychiatrists (AKAP) in the United States or at the Korean Neuropsychiatric Association in Seoul, respectively.

2) Presbyterian Endowment-funded Annual Lectureship on Social Justice and inclusiveness at the Davis Community Church, Davis, California.

3) K.W. Lee Journalistic Archive Endowment Fund at the University of California Davis (UCD) Shields Library and UCD Department of Asian American Studies. Any student and scholar writing a research paper on materials in the KW. Lee Archives would receive a small stipend scholarship.

Mr. K.W. Lee is a Korean American veteran journalist and winner of numerous national awards in investigative reporting. He is the only Asian American newspaper reporter inducted into the Newseum (a Hall of Fame for news reporters) located in Washington, DC. Mr. Lee was the publisher and editor-in-chief of a historical weekly newspaper, *Koreatown*, the only weekly English language Korean American newspaper existing in the early

1980s. K.W. Lee chronicled in detail the 1992 Los Angeles Rodney King Riots (Sa-ee-gu, "April 29") when several thousands of Korean American shops and stores were burned and destroyed.

4) National Defense Committee To Free Chol Soo Lee: a historical event in the Korean American immigration history.

Chol Soo Lee was a Korean American youth condemned to death-row in San Quentin for the 1973 murder of a gang member in San Francisco's Chinatown. After six months of investigation looking into the court trial documents, K.W. Lee was convinced that Chol Soo Lee was a victim of mistaken identity through racial profiling. What started as informal meetings at our home in Davis turned into the National Defense Committee to Free Chol Soo Lee. The committee appointed Mr. Jay Yoo, a UCD law school graduate as chairman of National Defense Committee. He later became a prominent national assemblyman in South Korea and is now a private practice lawyer in Korea. Grace served as the committee's vice chairwoman.

To our surprise, the committee's work, including a series of newspaper articles by K.W. Lee, hit the raw nerves of many Asian American college students and youth, and catapulted the spontaneous formation of grass-roots local defense committees nationwide. Students at UC Berkeley, UCLA, Harvard, Yale and Princeton established Chol Soo Lee defense committees. After seven years of retrials in court, Chol Soo Lee was finally released from prison in 1983.

This unprecedented Pan-Asian American, multigenerational national movement gave Asian Americans the confidence in achieving judicial justice. This movement served as a model for the next nationwide Pan Asian American protest movement seeking justice for Vincent Chin. Chinese American Vincent Chin was murdered in 1982 by two unemployed Detroit auto workers who mistakenly called Chin a "jap" and bludgeoned him to death with a baseball bat. After manslaughter pleas were entered, the judge granted each attacker two years probation with $3,700 fines without any jail time for Chin's murder!

The National Defense Committee (1978-1983) to free Chol Soo Lee condemned to death row in San Quentin for a murder crime he did not commit. Grass-roots defense movement sprung all over the country. After 5 years court battle, we won. Chol Soo was freed in March 1983 after 10 years imprisonment. Photos are parade demonstrating to free Chol Soo Lee.

This was the print of carved Christmas greeting card that I made for Chol Soo Lee movement supporters in 1981. Right side is the prison and the left side would be court and the pistol directed at Chol Soo Lee from the court. Chain is on the hand of Chol Soo Lee and there is a pigeon symbolizing peace.

Left side photo, Chol Soo Lee, his facial disfiguration is due to the third degree burn (2007). Right side photo, group photo of UCLA symposium on Chol Soo Lee (2008): from left, Chol Soo, Grace Kim, Mr. Wineglass (our first defense lawyer), Stuart Hanlon (2nd defense lawyer), Tink Thompson (investigator), Jay Yoo (Chair, Nationa Deefese Commitee to Fee Chol Soo Lee, (far right)

5) Establishment of the Luke and Grace Kim Endowed Professorship in Cultural Psychiatry at UCD Medical School.

I had been teaching and supervising psychiatric residents as a clinical professor of psychiatryat UC Davis (UCD) Medical School from its inception in the late 1960s until my retirement in 2006. In 1989, I initiated a seminar on "Culture, Ethnicity and Mental Health" for UCD psychiatric residents. Since then, there has been a geometrically rapid expansion in the UCD cultural psychiatry training program facilitated with the visionary foresight and support of Dr. Bob Hales, the department chairman. He established the Diversity Advisory Committee and recruited highly competent, productive core faculty members with ethnic minority backgrounds who are interested in cultural psychiatry and the cultural training program. UCD's Department of Psychiatry has become a nationally visible and recognized training center in cultural psychiatry receiving many awards for excellence.

Following our retirements, Grace and I began to down-size our lifestyle as the next chapter of our lives. We chose the Seal Beach retirement community in Southern California near where most of our children, grandchildren, and relatives live. We knew that our Davis house had appreciated greatly over the years and considered ways to use the sale proceeds. I was also concerned about the future of the cultural psychiatry program. At that time, I received word from Dr. Bob Hales through Dr. Russell Lim, chair of Diversity Advisory Committee, as to whether we would be interested in establishing an endowed professorship in cultural psychiatry in our names. Grace and I discussed the suggestion and it did not take us long to follow through with a "Yes!" We feel that the timing was more than a coincidence; it was almost perfect. We have been glad and very happy with our decision.

We were able to donate $250,000, which was matched with close to $1 million by the UCD Medical School. Thus, the Luke & Grace Kim Endowed Professorship in Cultural Psychiatry was established.

After an exhaustive search, Dr. Francis Lu, MD, Professor of Clinical Psychiatry at UCSF was selected and appointed to take the position beginning in July, 2009. We are very happy about Dr. Lu's selection because he has a great commitment and much to contribute to the cultural psychiatry program.

Dr. Lu is a nationally known, prominent cultural psychiatrist who has already accomplished a great deal in promoting cultural psychiatry. He spearheaded the adoption of mandatory training on ethnic minority mental health by all American psychiatric residency programs.

Establishment of the Luke and Grace Kim endowed Professorship in Cultural Psychiatry and Francis Lu, MD as the appointed Endowed Professor in Cultural Psychiatry

FRANCIS G. LU. M.D. the Luke and Grace Kim Professorship in Cultural Psychiatry.

Francis G. Lu, M.D., joined the UC Davis School of Medicine's Department of Psychiatry and Behavioral Sciences in July 2009 and serves as the department's director of cultural psychiatry and as associate director of the general psychiatry training program. He is also the director of training and dissemination for the Asian American Center for Disparities Research in the UC Davis Department of Psychology and has served on the State of California's Department of Mental Health Cultural Competence Advisory Committee since 1996. Dr. Lu's 33-year career has focused on cultural competence in healthcare for the increasingly diverse population of California; leadership for diversity activities within the University of California; reducing mental health disparities; psychiatric education, with an emphasis on recruitment and mentorship; and the interface of psychiatry with religion and spirituality.

He is the recipient of the American Psychiatric Association's 2001 Kun-Po Soo Award for his work in integrating Asian issues into psychiatry, the 2008 American Psychiatric Foundation's Advancing Minority Mental Health Award, and the Association for Academic Psychiatry's Lifetime Achievement in Education Award.

The Luke and Grace Kim Endowed Professorship in Cultural Psychiatry was established, in part, with a generous gift from the Kims in the hope that UC Davis will continue to serve as a nationally renowned and respected training and research center for cultural psychiatry. Dr. Luke Kim, a retired UC Davis clinical professor of psychiatry, gave annual seminars for psychiatry residents with the idea and conviction that beliefs and attitudes often affect the manifestation of mental illness and treatment.

[6-17] **Brief Comments about Grace:** Grace is a born

teacher. She had been a teacher/counselor in Korea and the United States for 35 years. She taught at Davis Senior High School for 24 years, from which she retired in 1996. She is widely known as a strong, effective community activist in Northern California as well as in southern Calif.

During her tenure at Davis High, Grace was instrumental in establishing the Human Relations Committee at every school in the Davis Joint Unified School District. She also established "Friendship Day" at Davis High, designed to improve the school climate and human relationships. Both of these programs were initiated in the wake of the 1983 racially motivated stabbing death of Thong Hy Huynh, a Vietnamese immigrant, on the Davis Senior High Campus.

Grace developed and taught a class called "Family Life and Personal Growth," which became a graduation requirement. The class covered communication skills and basic life management skills essential for present-day youth. She used role-play frequently to demonstrate and practice various situations and scenarios. The life management skills covered drug abuse, sex education, health management, anger management, stress management, time and finance management, and more.

In the community, Grace was an elder at the Davis Community Church and served on many General Assembly national committees of the Presbyterian Church, USA. She feels proud of being a product of the Ethnic Concerns Committee of the Sierra Mission Area, Presbyterian Church, USA, which was responsible for her own spiritual growth and leadership development. (For further detail, please refer to Appendix No. 12, Ethnic Concern Communities Article: Kim, Luke & Kim, Grace: Remember! Renew! Rejoice 30 Years of Racial Ethnic Advocacy in Sierra

Mission Area, Church & Society, Presbyterian Church (U.S.A.) Vol. 93 No. 3 pp 62-70, 2003)

Grace especially feels grateful for the opportunity to serve the Korean American Consulting Committee, Presbyterian Church USA, which worked with 350 Korean American churches in the United States by publishing Sunday school curriculum materials, a Korean American hymnal, and also sponsoring a continuing education program for ministers.

Grace was also politically involved. She played an active role in the campaign to elect Mary Chung Hayashi, the first Korean American woman elected to the California State Assembly. Grace worked with Mike Honda, then a California State Assemblyman, in passing the comfort women resolution through the California Assembly. After Honda became a U.S. congressman, he was instrumental in passing a federal version of the comfort women resolution as well as the establishment of Korean American Day.

Grace served on the national Board of Directors of the Korean American Coalition (KAC) including as vice chairperson for four years. She had been an active board member of CAPITAL (Council of Asian Pacific Islanders Together for Advocacy and Leadership). Grace has been an ongoing advisor to KAAN (Korean American Adoptee and Adoptive Family Network) for the last 20 years.

Now in retirement, she has been busier than ever. In 2009, she was the president of the Seal Beach Korean American Club. She also chaired the Staff and Parish Relations Team of Leisure World Community Church. Grace organized and founded the ongoing Annual Multicultural Festival at Seal Beach Leisure World. The Fourth Annual Multicultural Festival took place in October 2010, and was a great success. She also organized and founded the 30 member Korean American Chorale of Seal Beach Leisure World.

Prior to coming to Seal Beach, she served as Vice President and President of the Korean American Community Association of Greater Sacramento for two years in each position.

It will take a book to describe Grace's amazing life story. She has been the recipient of numerous awards and citations for her outstanding community and educational contributions (i.e. Teacher of the Year from PTA) and was honored with the "*Dong-Baekjang*" award which is the second highest Presidential medal awarded to civilians by the President of the Republic of Korea.

Left side photo is presidents of the ethnic clubs participating in 2010 4th annual multicultural festival. Grace Kim (MCC founder) is 3rd from the left. Right side photo members Korean American club participation at the Multi-Cultural Festival.

Grace is the founder of the annual Multicultural Festival at Seal Beach Leisure World beginning in 2007. This year's fourth annual festival was quite successful.

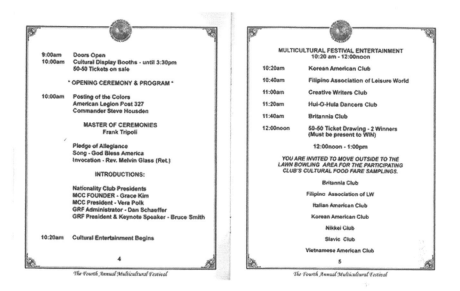

9:00am	Doors Open
10:00am	Cultural Display Booths - until 3:30pm
	50-50 Tickets on sale

* OPENING CEREMONY & PROGRAM *

10:00am	Posting of the Colors
	American Legion Post 327
	Commander Steve Housden

MASTER OF CEREMONIES
Frank Tripoli

Pledge of Allegiance
Song - God Bless America
Invocation - Rev. Melvin Glass (Ret.)

INTRODUCTIONS:

Nationality Club Presidents
MCC FOUNDER - Grace Kim
MCC President - Vera Polk
GRF Administrator - Dan Schaeffer
GRF President & Keynote Speaker - Bruce Smith

| 10:20am | Cultural Entertainment Begins |

4

The Fourth Annual Multicultural Festival

MULTICULTURAL FESTIVAL ENTERTAINMENT
10:20 am - 12:00noon

10:20am	Korean American Club
10:40am	Filipino Association of Leisure World
11:00am	Creative Writers Club
11:20am	Hui-O-Hula Dancers Club
11:40am	Britannia Club
12:00noon	50-50 Ticket Drawing - 2 Winners
	(Must be present to WIN)

12:00noon - 1:00pm

YOU ARE INVITED TO MOVE OUTSIDE TO THE
LAWN BOWLING AREA FOR THE PARTICIPATING
CLUB'S CULTURAL FOOD FARE SAMPLINGS.

Britannia Club

Filipino Association of LW

Italian American Club

Korean American Club

Nikkei Club

Slavic Club

Vietnamese American Club

5

The Fourth Annual Multicultural Festival

Program for the 2010 Multicultural Festival of Seal Beach Leisure World in which Grace Kim is identified as founder of MCC

Planning committee members from different ethnic clubs at 1st multicultural festival in 2007. Grace is 3rd from right front line.

This is Korean cultural booth in the 2010 annual multi-cultural festival of Seal Beach.

Seal Beach Korean American Chorale which was found by Grace Kim. Luke Kim is in back third person from the left.

Seal Beach Korean American Chorale men's group in 2009.

[6-18] Our children and grandchildren: Our two sons, David and Danny, have flourished in their professional lives.

[6-18 A] David Sung Chul Kim (김성철, 金聖喆):

Our older son, David was born May 17, 1963 in Vallejo, California and currently lives with his wife Julie(서쥴리, maiden name: 서시은, 徐智恩) and 2 children, Tessa (김신희, 金信喜)(17 years old) and Jaisohn (김신영, 金信榮) (15) in Vienna, Virginia.

In raising our children, there were many interesting stories, events and episodes. I will mention one event/episode for each son. The episode Grace and I vividly remember is a scene in which David was running a cross-country long distance race at Davis High. After a while, David was running far behind the pack. We thought he would give up and stop running in order to avoid embarrassment. To our surprise, he kept running all by himself toward the finish line, well after everyone else completed the race. He did not appear to mind that he was all alone, and he stayed with the event until he reached the end.

This episode illustrates his personality: steadiness, perseverance, and the determination to go forward until completion. David's personality reflects mine to some degree, and also reminds us of his grandpa who told us "Never give up!" We feel that David's character traits of steadiness and perseverance also reflect his career pattern.

David is a senior transportation professional with twenty-five years of experience at the local, state and federal level in the executive and legislative branches.

He received his BA in Political Science from Occidental College and a Master's Degree in Public Administration from the University of Southern California. Soon after graduating from Occidental College, he began to work for California State Senator David Roberti as a field representative. He then became an administrative assistant to California State Assemblyman Xavier Becerra, and when Becerra was elected to Congress, David followed him to D.C. to become his senior legislative assistant and key advisor on transportation, trade and health issues. From 1995 to 1998, he worked as Legislative Representative for the City of Los Angeles in its D.C. office. In April 1998, he was picked up by the Clinton administration and served as Deputy Assistant Trade Representative for Congressional Affairs. There he worked on various trade issues, and feels good about his key role in securing congressional passage of "Most Favored Nation" Trade Status for China. In March 1999, David became Deputy Director of the Washington D.C. Office for California Governor Gray Davis. When the Governor Davis' administration came to an end, David became Director of Federal Advocacy for the Los Angeles County Metropolitan Transportation Authority. In July 2008, he was promoted to Deputy Executive Officer, Federal Advocacy and Government Relations where he was successful in securing congressional approval for several transit projects. He is especially proud of the role he played in obtaining congressional approval of the $499 million Full Funding Grant for the Metro Gold Line East Side Light Rail Project.

In 2009, David was appointed to serve in the Obama Administration as Deputy Assistant Secretary for Governmental Affairs at the U.S. Department of Transportation. He said the job comes with long hours but he feels good about the position because of the opportunities to make a meaningful difference.

Julie has a BA in English from UCLA, and an MA from California State University Los Angeles. She was an English teacher at Davis High School, and with her journalism background, she publishes her church bulletin and other materials.

Julie is a descendant of Dr. Suh Jai Pil (서재필, 徐載弼) (Phillip Jaisohn M.D.), known as "the Jefferson of Korea." He could have been the first president of the Republic of Korea, but ceded the opportunity to later elected President Syngman Rhee. Dr. Jaisohn was a pioneer. In the1880's, he became the first naturalized U.S. citizen of Korean ancestry and he was also the first Korean American recipient of an M.D. degree from a U.S. medical school.

TESSA, DAVID, JULIE, JAISOHN

David Kim Elder Son in front of the capitol Washington DC

[6-18 B] Daniel Sungwoo Kim (김 성 우, 金聖):

Our younger son is Daniel. We call him Danny as he prefers to be called. Danny was born on May 23, 1965 at Kaiser Hospital in Vallejo, CA. He and his wife, Janet (이은경, 李恩炅), and their two children, Jeffrey (김신덕, 金信德, 11 years old) and Luke (김신우, 金信宇 8 years old) currently live in Encino (northern part of LA), California.

Danny's interest and favorite activities include music, audio engineering, and computers. He is an accomplished drummer, playing drums for the English-speaking ministry at Los Angeles' Young Nak Celebration Church near downtown Los Angeles. He was so good on drums that he won a highly coveted Louse Armstrong music award upon his graduation from Davis Senior High School. In fact, he said that after graduating, he wanted to go to Boston's Berklee School of Music (contemporary) where he wanted to major in drums. Both my wife and I have been pretty liberal, implying that we would allow our sons to choose whatever school and major they wanted. However, like many other Korean parents would do, we discouraged him from a major in music, but instead we wanted him to go into the computer sciences, which he had been very good at, as well as in music. In fact he was called as "an electronic handyman" in that if something goes wrong with a TV, computer, stereo, or recording devise, he can fix it without any difficulty. We discouraged music for the simple reason that the music field is highly competitive, and in reality, unless you are on the top as a world class drummer, it is difficult to survive economically. We further advised that if he preferred to, he could major in computer science with a minor in music. Luckily for us and for him, he chose to major in computer science. He applied for and was accepted for admission by California State University (CSU) Chico and University of the Pacific (UOP), a private college. After our campus visits to both campuses, he selected CSU Chico, because he favored their computer science department over that of UOP. He felt that Chico State had more active and advanced computer programs and activities and their computer program had a better reputation than that of UOP.

JEFFREY, DANNY, JANET, LUKE

We knew the chairman of the Department of Computer Science at Chico State who was a Filipino American professor married to a Korean female professor of Asian American History. We had met and known both professors from previous contacts. When we visited the Chico State campus and met the department chairman, he told us that he would welcome Danny into his Computer Science Department and added that he would take care of Danny by putting him under his wing. We felt doubly assured and relieved.

One episode about Danny I would like to describe is regarding a summer job he worked while he was still at Chico State University. A friend of mine who was the owner of a computer store in Sacramento offered a paid summer job to Danny, and added that he could receive certificates of completion of training on repairing printers and computers by working seriously and diligently in his computer store including actual repair work under his supervision on printers and computers. He was so happy for the opportunity and worked hard at the computer store for three months. At the end of his summer job, he actually received certificates of completion of training from the printer company, Epson. He told me later that his experience of working in the computer store taught him a lot about repairing computers and printers, and the certificates he received became the foundation from which he launched his career as a computer professional and advanced to his current career position as Director of Information Technology (IT.)

Behind the scene was my attempt to find ways to let Danny get deeply rooted into the world of computers. He did not find out until almost 15 years later that I had arranged with the owner to pay his salary for that summer job.

To this day Danny plays drum semi-professionally on top of his computer work as an IT director and seems to enjoy both worlds of computer and music very much. Grace and I feel very proud of Danny who has been a creative, innovative and hard-working IT Director with excellent people skills and as an outstanding drummer as well.

With his over 20 years of experience as and IT professional, he has been a reputable Director of IT in the field. He worked for such well-known companies as: BBDO West in LA, Goldberg Moser O'Neil of San Francisco, Fallon Worldwide of Minneapolis, MN, Saatchi & Saatchi / Publicis Groupe, Torrance, CA and Electronic Arts/Pandemic Studio, Los Angeles. Currently he works as a Global IT director of a computer company producing a computer games.

Danny and his wife, Janet, have two children, Jeffrey (10) and Luke (7) both of whom have been trained vigorously in *Wharang-Do* a Korean martial art which has a longer ancient history than that of Tae-Kwon Do. Janet is a Doctor of Oriental Medicine practicing Acupuncture and Herbal Medicine and has also been an examiner for the California Acupuncture Board.

[6-19] My life philosophy and bridge role between the East and West

I have been reflecting on the past 80 years of my life, especially as an Asian/ Korean Americanan psychiatrist over the last 40 years. I have been thinking how to summarize my life philosophy based on the totality of my experiences, thinking pprocesses, emotions, my values, and interpersonal relations, etc. Also I'd I like to think of myself as playing the role of a bridge between the East and West, and the last link between old Korean traditional values and the Americanized culture of our grandchildren, offspring and the younger Korean /Asian American/Pacific Islander (API) generations.

First of all, I must embrace the teachings of my father and Christianity as the main frame of reference. What I received from my parents are, of course, the heredity factors of DNA, and my father's personality characteristics: academically oriented seriousness in study and research; some of the Korean traditional values: peperseverance, tolerance and determination; and "while gentle and soft outside in appearance, strong, determined and persistent inside of the self."

What Christianity has taught me are: Bible and salvation; love your neighbor and service for others; a sense of gratitude, grace, forgiveness; every one is born equal before God and concepts of social justice. Also important are Christian-oriented western ideas of freedom, independence, democratic principles. I would like to explore more on methodology: 1) to introduce interesting and contrasting lives of the East and West, 2) to describe and show our struggles of life, survival, coping, pain and joy, and a life of *Jeong*.

I have listed below the emotional life I experienced and some of reasons behind these emotions as a Korean American immigrant psychiatrist.

1) Immigrant life in the US: as a medical intern trainee and psychiatric resident, I felt loneliness, homesickness, melancholy, moodiness, sense of isolation and marginality. Particularly I felt that I suffered from a lack of mentor and role model, I missed having someone whom I can look up and respect, and who are interested in my future and carrier development. Also during first one or two years, I had experienced some difficulty understanding certain colloquial English language (slangs). However, I do feel good, lucky and fortunate that I am bilingual because it gives me my appreciation of the richness of both English and Korean languages that provide

a complimentary roles helping me in searching and figuring out in my mind the most suitable, appropriate word/vocabulary in expression which may be lacking in one language vocabularies, whether it is English or Korean.

2) As a foreign medical graduate (FMG) and a young immigrant career psychiatrist, sometimes I felt unwelcome and unaccepted (at least non-verbally) by the mainstream professional community.

3) In psychiatric work pattern, there developed a 2-tier system of practice in American psychiatry: namely private practice psychiatry and public psychiatry. The majority of the U.S. Medical Graduate (USMG) American psychiatrists ignored the large segment of severely and/or chronically mentally ill population who were cared for in the state hospitals and public mental health clinics. Many American psychiatrists were interested in setting up plush private practices in fashionable locations, such as Beverly Hills, Boston or New York, doing psychotherapy with "neurotic" young, attractive, articulate, and "psychologically-minded" clients. However, I did observe that in recent years this kind of private practice pattern among the US Medical Graduates psychiatrists has declined with the demise in the popularity of long-term psychoanalysis and psychoanalytic psychotherapy.

Nevertheless, that is why public psychiatric clinics are desperate in recruiting physicians/psychiatrists. IMG (International Medical Graduates) psychiatrists have to fill the void and have become the' backbone of the psychiatric staff in American public psychiatry.

This kind of the 2-tier system of American Psychiatry apparently has led the American Medical Association (AMA) together with the Federal immigration policy to impose discriminatory practices sometimes in terms of opening and closing the door for IMGs to enter and receive the more desirable university residency programs than those of the non-university setting. For example, it was almost impossible for IMGs to be accepted by the university residency programs during 1950s to mid-1960s. However, following the Martin Luther King's civil rights movement and the advent of the Affirmative Action with more liberal policies, they opened up quite a bit in accepting IMGs to university resident programs. However, in the last 10 years or so, AMA together with Federal government closed down almost completely for IMGs the possibility of being accepted by the intern and residency programs in the U.S.

4) While I was in 4th year class in medical school, Prof. Nam Myung Suk, Chairman of the Psychiatry Department, Seoul National University Medical School was interested in me and guided me as my mentor. Prior to my graduation, we discussed intensively my future carrier plan and came to a mutual agreement regarding my graduate training in clinical phychology and psychiatric resident program in the U.S. so that I may return to Korea and become a faculty member of the medical school in order to establish a graduate program in clinical psychology in the medical school. Like a good soldier in carrying out General's order, I completed my graduate study with Ph.D. in clinical psychology at the University of Arizona (Tucson, AR) and a three year psychiatric residency program, and I was ready to return to Korea. As I mentioned already in this book, it was quite an unfortunate and sad disappointment for me that, due to the sudden premature death of Prof. Nam, I could not return to Korea because the promised faculty appointment and establishment of the clinical psychology program at SNU Medical School had not materialized. Under the circumstances, I had to give up my dream and decided to remain in the U.S.

Multi-religious environment of Korea: While in Korea, we have had frequent contacts with our neighbors and had opportunities to observe the people whose religions and religious life styles were different from ours as 3d generation Presbyterians. My observations led me to believe that each of different religions can offer uniquely positive aspects of viewpoints and wisdom. As a cultural psychiatrist, I try to understand them and integrate to find the commonality as well as the values each religion brings into.

I will summarize the positive aspects of each of religions, which are common in Asia, and our neighbors seem to have adopted. They are Christianity (40% of South Koreans are protestant or Catholic Christians) and Buddhism (30%).

However, Confucianism, Taoism, concept of Centering (Golden Middle) (중용,中庸) and Korean ethos are not religion, but are the philosophy of ways of life which contributed substantially to the foundation of the Korean traditional customs and value system including educational philosophy and social behavior.

However, I cannot forget that I grew up as a member of a 3rd generation Presbyterian family that has laid down western- oriented values on my otherwise Eastern values, more specifically, Far-East Asian values.

Christianity: One God only, Bible, Salvation, concept of Trinity; love your neighbor, concept of sacrifice and service for others; everyone is equal before God, social justice; gratitude, grace and forgiveness

Buddhism: Compassion, concept of inner tranquility and inner peace; meditation, yoga, emphasis on body-mind interaction and integration in health; "here and now" emphasis." Concept of greed and desire as the primary source of suffering and misery; Their Happiness formula: K ÷ greed/desire = happiness. (K = constant, limitations of reality); Concept of the reality as a personal illusion or personal projection.

Confucianism: Royalty, emphasis on interpersonal relationship (propriety) and social role; family values, respect for elders and ancestors; collectivistic orientation (we=woori= us vs. I, mine, me); Respect for education, scholarship, life-long learning; perseverance and determination; achievement of higher goals; intention and effort more important than spontaneity and natural ability; cognitive problem-solving more important than emotional expression of conflict and inner feelings; Service for public good and benevolence; and personhood/character development as a goal vs. critical thinking in US as the public school educational goal.

Taoism: to accept the Nature (vs. conquer and control the nature) and to live in harmony with the Nature.

Centering (중용,中庸): It denotes a golden middle, middle center, maintaining a balance with harmony, equilibrium and avoiding the extremes of the right and left, the bipolar ends of the pole. No matter how good it is (i.e., love, money, health, food, etc.) If it is too good in an extreme way, it becomes no good already. Thus to avoid the extreme is very important, no matter how good the subject matter is. In addition, the basic philosophy of Oriental medicine is that health is based on good balance and harmony of the different organs.

My final word: "Pursuit of happiness is like grabbing in the fog; usually happiness ensues afterward as a result of meaningful work and experience, and not attained because happiness is pursued."

At this stage of my life after 40 years of practice of psychiatry and psychology in the US, my current orientation can be described as "A life-long journey and quest of eclectic complementary synthesis, integration and development of the East and the West traditions" in the practice and theory of psychotherapy, which has been on-going process.

Finally, I would like to express my appreciations and thanks to the United States, especially for their educational systems, for the generosity for foreign students. In my case, I received excellent education and training in clinical psychology at the University Arizona with a scholarship.

[6-20] Final Word

1) I've gone through difficult periods and traveled rather bumpy roads in my life. In particular, we experienced difficulty coping under the Japanese colonial occupation of Korea, especially toward the end of World War II, and our lives under Kim IL Sung's Communist Government from which we escaped to South Korea, and then the highly destructive Korean War itself!! I encountered many narrow escapes from death, such as my hiding underground to avoid detection by North Korean agents, the kidnapping of my mother from whom we have not heard for 60 years, my profound experience of the Hungnam Evacuation, and our miserable refugee life in a tent at a refugee camp, Busan, and so forth. And then I came to the United Sates, where I encountered racial prejudice and discrimination personally as well as professionally. As an immigrant Asian-American psychiatrist, I was treated as a second class professional in the medical professional community.

In spite of these crisis and the adverse environment, I was able to survive and overcome, and eventually became stronger in resiliency and character, perseverance, my strong will and determination to overcome and eventually succeed.

In reviewing my past life, I believe I developed a more resilient and stronger character because of (a) my strong faith in God who has given me hope and an increased capacity for love and tolerance, (b) the pure, abiding love of Grace, my wife, with our life-long sharing of camaraderie and the same life goals, (c) the mutual trust, selfless love and blood-related solidarity our parents and siblings have had for each other, and (d) many unforgettable relatives and friends who have shared with me their enduring and supportive *Jeong*-rich relationships. (e) Also I must mention the role that music has played in my life, especially classical music, such as that of Bach, Beethoven and Mozart that helped me grow spiritually, and gave me strength and peace of mind.

2) In looking back over almost 50 years of our life together, both Grace and I agree that we have had relatively solid, steady, stable, and generally happy lives. I am sure that our 36 year continuous residence at the same Davis house added to a sense of stability.

Since we moved to Seal Beach Leisure World, Grace has experienced some difficulty adjusting to the new environment. She feels that Davis has been her home and her hometown, where she lived the longest time, for 36 years, much longer than any other place she ever lived in her entire life. Therefore she misses Davis very much. Although I have been adjusting reasonably well to Seal Beach Leisure World, I don't blame her for missing Davis so much because I agree with her view of Davis.

She had been very actively involved in the Davis community socially, professionally and politically. She taught at Davis Sr. High school for 24 years, during which she made some important contributions to the Davis school system. For example, through the Board of City Councils, she was instrumental in establishing and setting up the Human Relations Committee in each and every school in the Davis Unified School District. She was an active member of the Davis Community Church as a church leader. Davis is a liberal university town of about 50,000-60,000 population, about half of which are UC Davis undergraduate and graduate students. Relatively separated from neighboring towns geographically, Davis is a very friendly community, where musical and artistic activities are high, just as the average educational level of Davis residents is pretty high. Grace indicated to me that she likes the weather here much better than in Davis and the weather here is almost ideal. However, she added that the heavy traffic on freeways and the faces of old folks only, without any young children's face in Leisure World cause her some unhappiness

3) In general, each of us had been working hard and diligently, and we were highly productive, making contributions to our community and to each of our own professions, which gave us a sense of excitement and enthusiasm toward life.
4) I feel that I am a very lucky man to have married Grace as she has been a wonderful, exceptional wife to me. I am especially grateful to

Grace for looking after me in all aspects of the knit-gritty details of my physically disabling health and daily schedules, including helping me publish both the Korean and English versions of my autobiography.

5) We are very thankful to God for the fact that our children and grandchildren are healthy physically, mentally and spiritually and that God has blessed our family greatly and abundantly both individually and collectively as a family.

My final word is that I am well aware of my physical disability due to the slow progression of Parkinson's disease which is affecting my general health and work efficiency. It is becoming increasingly difficult for us to maintain the same life style, orientation and our life goal.

I feel that we need to modify our life's priority: to live day by day with thankfulness, gratitude, honesty, diligence and integrity. And the most important task left for us to do is *to take care of our own health until God calls us.*

Reference

Acheson, Dean: The Korean War. New York, W.W. Norton, 1971

Chung, D: Three Day Promise: a Korean Soldier's Memoir. Tallahasse FL, Father & Son Pub. 1989

Hastings, Max: The Korean War. New York, Simon, & Schuster, 1987

Kim, Luke & Kim, Grace: Remember! Renew! Rejoice 30 Years of Racial Ethnic Advocacy in Sierra Mission Area, Church & Society, Presbyterian Church (U.S.A.) Vol. 93 No. 3 pp 62-70, 2003

Lee, Ki-Baik: A New History of Korea. Translated by Wagnor, E. Cambridge, MA, Harvard University Press, 1984

Solberg, SE: The Land and People of Korea. New York, HarperCollins, 1991

Pictures

Grace and Luke 2008

David our eldest son was born in 1963

David

David

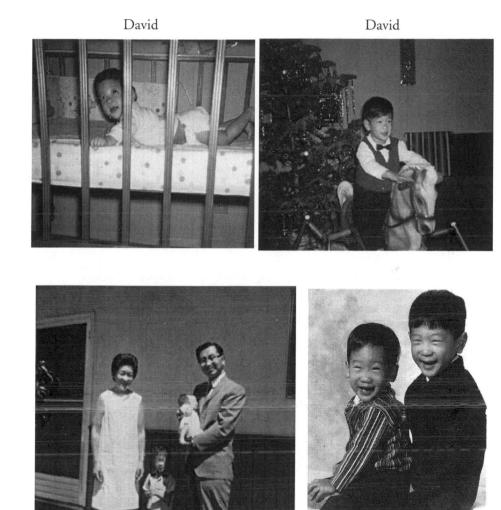

Danny our second son was born and came
home from the hospital
in Vallejo in 1965

Danny and David

Family snapshot in front of Stanford University Medical Center

Our family with Grace's mother, Mrs. Song, in San Luis Obispo home at
Christmas time in 1969

Family Photo at Davis (1973) front left side is Danny and left back is David.

Grandfather and family are looking over the albums in Davis 1975.

Family at house Backyard, Davis California.

David and Julie's wedding in 1987 in LA.

Tessa, first child of David and Julic.

Younger son Danny's Wedding Day After the wedding, they had Korean traditional wedding ceremony. (1997)

Danny's family with his two sons, Jeffery and Luke in 2004.

Jeffery and Luke pay respect to their grandparents with New Year's greeting.

They are happy after receiving Sae baet Don (best wishes money).

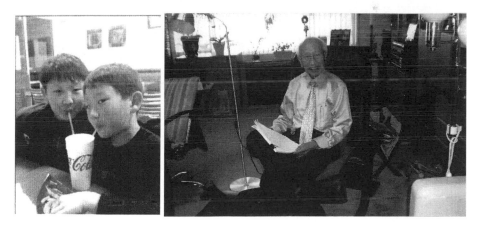

Danny's two children, Jeffery and Luke. Luke at his living room.

Family back home in Seoul Korea including sister Ik Nan's family at her home.

Graveyard of Luke's father and stepmother in Davis, CA.

With sister Ik Nan at the tomb of my grandmother Young Hwa Kim in Youngnak cemetery in Seoul.

In front of Dr. Philip Jaisohn's (Soh, Jae-Pil) 1866–1951, tombstone at National Cementery, Seoul, Korea. First Korean American Medical doctor, graduate of George Washington Medical School and leader in the Korean indendence movement in the USA.

Four grandchildren. From left Jaisohn, Jeffrey, Luke, and Tessa.

Jeffrey and Luke are performing Hwarang-do martial art at the grandfather's 80th birthday party in October, 2010.

Grace, her family and activities

Jae Woong Chun Grace's father. (1902–1963)

From right to left Grace's mother Mrs. Sung Do Song, 1909–2001
Grace, Grace's sister Kay, Grace's niece Shannon.

Grace graduating from Cal Poly San Luis Obispo with master's
degree in educational counseling in 1969.

Grace delivering nominating speech for GA moderator at Presbyterian Church
USA General Assembly in Phoenix Arizona in 1984.

Grace received Dong Baek Jang the second highest civilian medal awarded by the President of the republic of Korea. The award was delivered by Council General Jong Hoon Kim in San Francisco.

Grace as President of the Korean Community Association of Greater Sacramento greeting the President Kim Dae Joong in San Francisco in 2000.

Grace at the reception for the President Noh Moo Hyun in 2004.
Second from the left is Grace.

Celebrating Grace's published book in LA (1988), Jay Yoo, MC, at far left

Grace's Book signing event. 1988

Sookmyung alumni at the Grace's book publication celebration party.

Some Luke's Activities

Attending professional meetings

The 3rd scientific meeting of the Pacific Rim College of Psychiatrists in Tokyo, Japan in 1986.

THE 3RD SCIENTIFIC MEETING OF THE PACIFIC RIM COLLEGE
OF PSYCHINATRISTS   TOKYO, JAPAN APRIL 2~5, 1986

THE 3RD SCIENTIFIC MEETING OF THE PACIFIC RIM COLLEGE
OF PSYCHINATRISTS   TOKYO, JAPAN APRIL 2~5, 1986

The 4th scientific meeting of the Pacific Rim College of Psychiatrists in Hong
Kong in 1988

Luke Kim in podum Scientific Conference in Seoul Korea in 1993.

Celebrating Luke's retirement in 1996.

With congressman Robert Matsui who was invited to Sacramento Korean American Association as keynote speaker when Grace was the president of the association in 1998.

Surrounded by Hawaiian beauties in 2003.
Centennial Celebration of Korean Immigration to USA.

Well known singer Young Nam Cho who helped Choul Soo Lee defense
committee. Far right is K W Lee investigative reporter who worked with us in
the Choul Soo Lee movement.

Appendix

1. APA Psychiatric News Article on Dr. Luke Kim by Pychiatric News Reporter Eva Bender

Highlights of My Life and the Korean War Story: Hungnam Evocation, Ship of Miracles a Beyound (Eve Bender wrote the complete life stories of Luke Kim succinctly only in four pages and printed here in the APA Psychiatric News dated October 17, 2009).

After coming of age amidst a vortex of political strife, government oppression, and personal loss, psychiatrist Luke Kim, M.D., Ph.D., has used his knowledge and experience to help his peers in the mental health profession to better understand the backgrounds of their patients.

Though he is retired, his legacy as a pioneer in the teaching of cultural psychiatry lives on through the Luke and Grace Kim Endowed Professorship in Cultural Psychiatry in the department of psychiatry at the University of California Davis School of Medicine. Kim established the professorship in 2006 with $250,000 of his own funds from the sale of his house in Davis. The University more than doubled funding toward the endowment.

Kim and his wife of 47 years, Grace, now live in a large retirement community in Seal Beach, Calif., and have two sons and four grandchildren.

After a multiyear search, Francis Lu, M.D., in July 2009 took the position as the Luke and Grace Kim Endowed Professor in Cultural Psychiatry in the UC Davis department of psychiatry & behavioral sciences, where he is also the director of cultural psychiatry and associate director of residency training.

Lu was formerly a professor of clinical psychiatry at the University of California, San Francisco, and director of the Cultural Competence and Diversity Program in the psychiatry department at San Francisco General Hospital.

"Luke and Grace are very warm people who are dedicated to furthering the field of cultural psychiatry," Lu told Psychiatric News in an interview. "With this endowment, they have extended Luke's legacy to future generations of psychiatrists," he said.

Kim was born in 1930 in the harbor city of Shinuiju, now North Korea as the oldest of four children. When Kim was five, the family moved to Tokyo so that his father could pursue a university degree in civil engineering. When his father was hired as the civil engineer for the regional province government in North Korea three years later, the family moved back.

Kim attended a private school in North Korea, a country then occupied by Japan. At the time, all public and private schools in Korea were under Japanese authority, and Kim was one of many students required to participate in daily military marches, drills, and other activities. "We were forbidden to speak Korean in school," Kim recalled in an interview with Psychiatric News.

At the age of 14, Kim, along with about 300 other peers from his school, was taken by train away from home under the order of the Japanese military in order to do forced hard labor. The boys were "interned" in a Japanese weapons factory that was surrounded by 10 foot high cement walls topped with barbed wire and the camp was heavily guarded. "The Pyongyang factory looked like a prison compound," Kim said. Kim and his peers manufactured bombs, machine guns, and other weapons for long hours every day, were fed rice with pieces of turnip, and slept on the bare wooden barracks floor.

On the morning of August 15, 1945, the boys were called to assemble in a large space, where they heard the Japanese Emperor Hirohito reading the text of an unconditional surrender in a shaky voice, according to Kim. It was the day that they would leave the camp for the first time in 14 months.

When Kim returned to school, a Japanese ROTC officer assigned to the school, ashamed that the Japanese Imperial Army surrendered and thus was defeated in the war, first killed his pregnant wife and then shot with his own pistol, which was found lying near his body.

The officer's body was cremated, and Kim, as student body president, was chosen to pick up the cremated bones from the ashes with chopsticks. "It was a task I performed with unforgettable feelings of eerie sadness," he said.

North Korea fell under communist rule after World War II ended and many families, in an attempt to escape the oppressive new government, crossed the 38th parallel to find new lives in South Korea. "This exodus brought about much tragedy for many," including his own family, Kim said, because relatives became separated permanently.

Kim's uncle, a Presbyterian minister, was kidnapped and imprisoned for his Christian beliefs and later sent to a labor camp near Siberia. Kim doesn't know what became of his uncle or many other relatives— after that. "I still have many aunts, nephews, and cousins living in North Korea and I have not been able to establish contact with them since 1946," he said.

Kim's father learned from a friend that he was about to be arrested for practicing his Christian faith and so moved the family successfully across the 38th parallel to South Korea. "Freedom of religion was important to us and was one of the reasons we fled," Kim said.

In Seoul, South Korea, Kim completed high school and entered Seoul National University College of Liberal Arts and Science as a premed student, where he met his future wife, Grace. Grace was then studying to become a teacher at the University.

One of the foundations of Luke and Grace's relationship was their Christian faith and their work in the Presbyterian Church.

Life was not without its difficulties, however. During the Korean War, Kim's mother was kidnapped from their house by North Korean authorities, most likely due to the fact that she was a leader in the Presbyterian Church. Kim later learned that during this time period, many Koreans were forced to walk 200 miles to North Korea on foot, and if they lived, were imprisoned there. On the long march, however, many became weak and died, or were shot to death if they walked too slowly.

"The last day I saw my mother was August 28, 1950," Kim said. Since that time, Kim has made multiple attempts to learn about her fate through the International Red Cross, but has been unsuccessful thus far.

Kim graduated from Seoul National University School of Medicine in 1956 and under the advice of a professor there, entered a clinical psychology program at the University of Arizona with the intention of returning to South Korea to start a new clinical psychology program in the medical school. However, Kim's mentor passed away shortly before his expected return to Korea. Therefore he decided to remain in the US and asked Grace to come to America to marry him. At that time. Grace had a busy life as she was teaching at a high stool during the day time, and in the evening, she organized and established an evening vocational high school for homeless, orphaned teenagers, with her volunteer teacher friends. Indeed, she did come to the US, leaving whatever she was doing behind her in Korea. Finally they got married in Buffalo in 1962 following a long 6 year courtship of weekly exchanges of letters across the Pacific Ocean. At that time Luke was going through a psychiatric residency training at the University of Buffalo and Buffalo State Hospital.

Following residency, Luke and Grace moved to California and after completing a psychiatric internship at Mt. Zion Hospital in San Francisco, began working at the Department of Corrections California Medical Facility in Vacaville, Calif., where from 1970 to 1982 he served first as senior psychiatrist and coordinator, and then chief of professional education and chief psychiatrist. During that time, Kim worked with such infamous prisoners as Charles Manson and Sirhan Sirhan. One of his inmate research assistants he hired was Timothy Leary, a former Harvard psychology professor, and "a LSD guru" who was in prison for drug charge. Kim described as "a visionary." talking about outer space planetary much ahead of his time.

He joined the faculty at the UC Davis department of psychiatry 1973 and in 1996 became a clinical professor. During his tenure there, in 1979, Kim established the Association of Korean Psychiatrists.

A decade later, Kim began teaching a seminar on cultural psychiatry to UC Davis psychiatry residents each year. He also authored an academic paper called "Korean Ethos" which was presented at an American Academy of Psychoanalysis conference in 1994 and subsequently won APA's Kun-Po Soo award for the paper, which describes the major principles of Korean ethos which were largely unfamiliar to American psychiatrists at the time. The paper, for instance, explored a value held by many Koreans is the importance of "Che-myun," the concept of face-saving in order to maintain dignity and respect.

In his annual seminar, Kim taught psychiatry residents and medical students about the cultural backgrounds of Asian American patients and how prevailing beliefs and attitudes and backgrounds often affect the manifestation of mental illness and treatment.

He rallied faculty in the department of psychiatry with diverse cultural backgrounds to teach their students about the cultural backgrounds of African American and Latino patients as well.

With the leadership and foresight of Robert Hales, M.D., MBA, Professor and Chairman of the Department of Psychiatry at UC Davis Medical School, recruited young dedicated new faculty interested in cultural psychiatry, and established a Diversity Advisory Committee, which facilitated the rapid growth of cultural psychiatry in the Department, this won an award in 2007 from the American College of Psychiatrists.

The committee members ensured that cultural psychiatry courses were incorporated into the mainstream curriculum. With the establishment of the Luke and Grace Kim Endowed Professorship in Cultural Psychiatry, Kim hopes that UC Davis will continue to serve as a nationally-renowned and highly respected training and research center for cultural psychiatry, he remarked.

Although he retired from his post at UC Davis more than three years ago, Kim and his wife, Grace, have never stopped their mission of teaching others about culture.

Two years ago, Grace organized the first multicultural festival in their retirement community of nearly 10,000 residents. It has now become an annual event attended by many of the residents. The festival features keynote speakers, cultural display booths of different ethnic clubs, a copious amount of international food, and traditional music and dance performed by people of diverse backgrounds.

"We share so many cultures here," Grace told Psychiatric News. "We have so much to learn about one another and to learn how to live together in peace and harmony by appreciating the true meaning of diversity among us."

2. Curriculum Vitae of Luke Ik-Chang Kim

Luke I.C. Kim, M.D.
1781 Sunningdale Road, 48A
Seal Beach, CA 90740
562-431-3039
lukek62@gmail.com.

EDUCATION:

1943:   Graduated from Wakadake Elementary School, Sinuiju, North Korea
1943:   Entered Osan Middle School
1945:   Transfer to Dong Joong (East) Middle School, Sinuiju, North Korea
1946:   Transfer to Seoul High School, Seoul, Korea
3/49:   Graduated from Seoul High School as the 1st graduating Class
4/49-3/52:   Seoul National University, Seoul, Korea, Pre-medical Diploma
4/52-3/56:   Seoul National University School of Medicine (M.D.)
9/56-6/60:   University of Arizona, Tucson, Arizona (Ph.D. in Clinical Psychology)

POST-DOCTORAL PROFESSIONAL TRAINING:

7/56-6/57:   Rotating internship, St. Mary's Hospital and Pima County Hospital, Tucson, AZ
7/60-6/61:   Post-doc internship in clinical psychology, Buffalo State Hospital, Buffalo, NY
7/61-3/63:   Psychiatric residency, Buffalo State Hospital, Buffalo, NY
7/65-6/66:   Rotating internship, Mt. Zion Hospital, San Francisco, CA
7/66-12/67:   Psychiatric residency, Napa State Hospital, Napa, CA (CDC Career Psychiatric Residency program)
1/67-6/67:   California Community Mental Health Training Center, Berkeley, CA

PROFESSIONAL EXPERIENCE:

3/63-6-65:	Staff psychologist, California Medical Facility (CMF), Vacaville, CA
1/68-1/70:	Staff psychiatrist, CMC-E, San Luis Obispo, CA
1/70-1/80:	Senior psychiatrist, Coordinator of Research and Staff Development, California Medical Facility, Department of Corrections, Vacaville, CA
1/80-2/82:	Chief of Professional Education, CDC Career Psychiatric Residency, Department of Corrections California Medical Facility, Vacaville, CA
2/82-2/84:	Chief psychiatrist, California Medical Facility, Vacaville, CA
3/84-11/97:	Senior psychiatrist, Parole Outpatient Clinic, California Department of Corrections, Sacrament, CA
8/97:	Recipient of the State Department of Corrections Director's Community Service Award
5/75-2005:	Staff psychiatrist (part-time), Yolo County Department of Alcohol, Drug and Mental Health Services, Woodland, CA
10/95-11/06:	Staff psychiatrist (part-time), Visions Unlimited, South Sacramento Mental Health Services, Sacramento, CA
3/97-10/05:	Staff psychiatrist (part-time), Northgate RST Mental Health Services, Turning Point, Sacramento, CA (clinic of the psychiatric residency training site of UC Davis School of Medicine)

ACADEMIC TEACHING AND AFFILIATION:

1973-1996:	Clinical instructor, assistant clinical professor, and associate clinical professor of psychiatry, UC Davis School of Medicine
7/96-10/05:	Clinical Professor of Psychiatry, UC Davis School of Medicine
7/96:	Recipient of the Distinguished Service Award of the Department of Psychiatry, UC Davis, School of Medicine
7/96-2003:	Research Professor of Psychology, National Research Center on Asian American Mental Health, Department of Psychology, UC Davis (Stanley Sue, Ph.D., Director)

5/1997:   Recipient of the 1997 Asian American Award (Kun-Po Soo Award) of the American Psychiatric Association, (APA) Annual Convention, San Diego, CA. 1997

6/2006:   Establishment of the Luke and Grace Kim Endowed Professorship in Cultural Psychiatry in the Department of Psychiatry, UC Davis School of Medicine.

2/2007:   American College of Psychiatrists' annual award for Innovation and Creativity in psychiatric education (award given to the Diversity Advisory Committee—Luke Kim's contributions to the committee as an originator of seminar courses in cultural psychiatry in UC Davis psychiatric department)

PROFESSIONAL MEMBERSHIP, CERTIFICATES & OFFICER ACTIVITIES:

- California Medical License (4/68): A 22070

- Board certification (# 16485, 7/77) by American Board of Psychiatry and Neurology, Inc.

- DEA Registration No: #AK0071530

- Distinguished Life Fellow, American Psychiatric Association (APA)

- Member of AMA, CMA, Sacramento Medical Society, Central CA Psychiatric Society, etc.

- Member of APA Taskforce on Asian American Psychiatrists (1972)

- Member of APA Committee of Asian American Psychiatrists (1973-1983)

- Editor-in-Chief, APA Asian American Psychiatrists Newsletter (1975-1983)

- Founding president (1979-1982), The Association of Korean American Psychiatrists. Reviewer, American Journal of Psychiatry (in 1980s)

PROFESSIONAL/COMMUNITY ACTIVITIES & CONSULTATION SERVICES:

11/79-5/80: Consultant, HEW project on mental health training curriculum on ethnic minorities, US Department of Health, Education and Welfare, Washington, DC.

1/79-3/80: Consultant, Task force on crime, violence and prison system, National Institute of Law Enforcement and Criminal Justice, Department of Justice, Washington, D.C.

9/80-2/84: Training Consultant, Richmond-Maxi Mental Health Services, San Francisco, CA

9/80-3/83: Consultant and teaching faculty, the National Training Center for Asian Pacific Clinical Psychology, San Francisco, CA

2/81-2/82: Member, Task force on Asian Pacific mental health, California State Department of Mental Health

2/85-3/86: Member, Asian Pacific Advisory Board, California State Department of Education

10/92-5/93: Consultant, the Health Work Group on urban violence, Center for Substance Abuse Prevention, US Department of Health and Human Services, Washington, DC.

1/82-2004: Charter Board member and psychiatric training consultant, Asian Pacific Community Counseling Services, Sacramento, CA

3/94-2005: Member, Board of Directors, Friends of Korea, and Korean Culture and Language Institute, Korean Adoptee and Adoptive Family Network (KAAN), etc.

7/96-6/98: President, Board of Directors, Korean American Community Association of Greater Sacramento

5/97-5/01: Member, National Advisory Council, Center for Substance Abuse Prevention, Substance Abuse Mental Health Service Administration (SAMHSA), US Department of Health and Human Services

5/98: Visiting lecturer, FBI Training Academy, Quantico, VA

7/98-2/99:   Member, Initial Review Group (IRG) of Federal Grant Proposals, Substance Abuse and Mental Health Services Administration (SAMHSA), US Department of Health and Human Services, Washington, DC.

7/03-1/05:   Director, Noin-Gungang Health Information Center (Funded by CA Endowment, Sacramento, CA

PUBLICATIONS / MAJOR PRESENTATIONS:

-   "A Study of Bender-Gestalt Tests with Different Clinical Groups," Ph.D. dissertation, University of Arizona June 1 1960

-   "Psychiatric Services Integrated into the California Correctional System," International Journal of Offender Therapy, Vol. 15, No.3, 1971

-   "Long-term Use of Lithium in Aggressive Prisoners," with Joe Tupin, et al. Comprehensive Psychiatry, Vol. 1, No. 14, July/August, 1973

-   "Psychotherapy with Black Offenders," presented at the American Psychiatric Association Convention, Detroit, MI, May 1974

-   "Issues in group psychotherapy with character-disordered prisoners," California Department Corrections Research Monograph, No. 56, 1973

-   "Effectiveness of group psychotherapy with prisoners," presented at the American Psychiatric Association Convention, Miami, FL, May 1976

-   "Research Problems with Asian Pacific Population," presented at the American Psychiatric Association Annual Convention, Toronto, Canada, May 1977

-   "Psychosocial Development of Korean American Children," a chapter in "Psychosocial Development of Minority Children," edited by Johnson-Powell, Morales, Yamamoto, J. Brunner-Mazel, NY, 1979

- The Korean language translation of the questionnaires of "*Psychiatric Status Schedule*" (research diagnostic manual) by Robert Spitzer, et al. A UCLA project with Joe Yamamoto, MD, 1979

- "A Study on the Predication of Violence Potential," a paper presented at the First Pacific Congress of Psychiatry, Manila, Philippines, May 1980

- "Mental Health of Southeast Asian refugees," a panel presentation at the American Psychiatric Association Annual Convention, San Francisco, CA, May 1980

- "The Role of Chae-Myun (face-saving) in Koreans' Interpersonal Behavior," a panel presentation at the 3rd Scientific Conference of the Pacific Rim College of Psychiatrists, Seoul, Korea, May, 1984

- "Mental Health of Korean American Elderly," with C. Kiefer, et al., the Journal of Gerontological Society of America, Vol.25, No.5, 1985, USHHS Research Grant, No. MH34334, Final Report, June 1983

- Member (1986-1990), Editorial Board, Newsletter of International Medical Graduate Psychiatrists

- "A Study of Korean American Immigrant Elderly," a paper presented at the joint scientific conference of the University of California and Seoul National University Departments of Psychiatry, Seoul, Korea, April 1986

- "Korean American Immigrants and their Adjustment Processes," a paper presented at the Center for Korean Study, University of California, Berkeley, CA, Feb. 1989

- "Korean Ethos: Concept of Jeong and Haan," presented at the American Academy of Psychoanalysis, San Antonio, TX, Dec. 1990

- "Psychiatric Care of Korean Americans," a chapter in "*Culture, Ethnicity and Mental Illness*," edited by A. Gaw, American Psychiatric Press, 1992

- "Transition Generation: Korean American Young adults," a paper presented at the San Francisco Bay Area Korean American Coalition Conference, Oct 1992; also published in "The mental health of Asian Americans," presented at 6th Scientific Conference of the Pacific Rim College of Psychiatrists, Shanghai, China, April 1993

- "The physical and mental Health of Korean Immigrants in the USA," presented at the World Congress of Korean Psychiatrists, the Korean Neuropsychiatric Association, October 22, 1993, Seoul, Korea.

- "Preventive Mental Health for Asian Immigrant Elderly," presented at the Community Forum, sponsored by Asian Pacific Community Counseling, Sacramento, CA, April 1994

- "Korean American Identity," a paper presented at KASCON VIII (the National Conference of Korean American College Leadership), Philadelphia, PA February, 1994

- "Korean American Immigrants and Their Children," a monograph, New Faces of Liberty, A Zellerbach Family Fund Project, Many Cultures Publishing, San Francisco, May, 1994

- "The Mental Health of Asian American Women," presented at the third Scientific Conference of the Global Awareness Society International, June 4, 1994, Chicago, IL

- "The physical and mental Health of Asian Pacific American Retirees," presented at the Filipino Community Forum, sponsored by Asian Pacific Community Counseling, Sacramento, CA June 11, 1994

- "Beyond the Ego: Psychotherapy and Spirituality," a paper presented at the California Society of the Association of Korean American Psychiatrists, (AKAP), San Pedro, CA, Oct. 10, 1994

- "Psychotherapy with Asian American Clients," a paper presented at the 2nd Annual Conference of Harbor-UCLA and Los Angeles County Department of Mental Health, Oct., 1996

- "Korean Ethos," Journal of Korean American Medical Association (KAMA), Number 1, p13-23, 996

- "Korean American Children - with Kim, WJ, $ Rue, D. a chapter in "Transcultural Child Psychiatry," edited by Johnson-Powell, G. and Yamamoto, J. Wiley & Sons Publisher, NY, 1997

- "Asian Cultures and Psychotherapy," Asian American Award lecture (Kun—Po Soo Award), APA Annual Scientific Convention, San Diego, CA May 20, 1997

- "Evaluating and Understanding Asian Americans in forensic setting," with Stanley Sue "Child Psychiatry," edited by Johnson-Powell, G. and Yamamoto, J. Wiley & Sons Publisher, NY, 1997

- "Asian Cultures and Psychotherapy," Asian American Award lecture (Kun—Po Soo Award), APA Annual Scientific Convention, San Diego. CA May 20, 1997

- "Evaluating and Understanding Asian Americans in forensic setting," with Stanley Sue, Workshop sponsored by California Forensic Mental Health Association, San Francisco, CA, October, 1997

- Publication of the Korean translation of "Transpersonal Psychotherapy" (488 pages) by Seymour Boorstein, MD, with Seung Douk Cheung, MD, Oct. 1997. Hana Medical Book Publisher, Seoul, Korea

- "Searching for and defining a Korean American identity in a multicultural society," with Kim, Grace, a chapter in Korean American Women: From Tradition to Modem Feminism, edited by Young 1. Song and Alice Moon, Praeger Publisher, Westport, CT, 1998

- "The mental health of Korean American women," a chapter in "Korean American Women: From Tradition to Modem Feminism," edited by Young 1. Song and Alice Moon, Prgaeger Publisher, Westport, CT.1998

- "Transpersonal psychology in the context of Korean culture," a paper presented at the 9th scientific convention of the Pacific Rim College of Psychiatrists, Oct. 3, 1999, Seoul, Korea

- "To name our feelings: searching out Korean psychology, ethos, and emotions." Korean Quarterly Vol. 3 No.4, St Paul, iv1N, 2000

- Publication of the Korean translation of "Clinical Studies in Transpersonal Psychotherapy" by Seymour Boorstein, MD, with Seung Douk Cheung, MD, March, 2001 Sujo Publisher, Seoul, Korea

- "The concept of Jeong and Haan and its psychotherapeutic application," a paper presented at Symposium, American Psychiatric Association annual convention, San Francisco, May 22, 2003

- Seminar course on "Culture and ethnicity in psychiatry" 12 weeks yearly (1990-2001) for psychiatric residents at the University of California Davis Medical Center, Sacramento, CA

- Seminar course on "Religious and spiritual aspects of health and healing," 6 weeks yearly (1999 to 2000) for psychiatric residents at the University of California Davis Medical Center, Sacramento, CA

- Publication of the Korean translation (2ed) of "Clinical Studies in Transpersonal Psychotherapy" by Seymour Boorstein, MD, with Seung Douk Cheung, MD. August, 2005, Hana Medical Book Publisher, Seoul, Korea

- Presentation of paper," Current status, issues and psychiatric residency training in religion, spirituality and transpersonal subjects in American psychiatry," at Scientific Convention Korean Neuro-psychiatric Association, Oct, 21-23, 2005, Seoul, Korea

41st CONVOCATION OF FELLOWS

Monday, May 19, 1997
7:30 p.m.
Manchester Ballrooms D-I
Second Floor
Hyatt

Luke I. C.
Kim, M.D., Ph.D.

KUN-PO SOO AWARD*(Asian-American Award)

Luke I. C. Kim, M.D., Ph.D., received his medical degree from Seoul National University School of Medicine, Korea, and a doctoral degree in clinical psychology from the University of Arizona in Tucson. He did his internship and psychiatric residency training at Buffalo State Hospital, Mt. Zion Hospital and Medical Center in San Francisco and Napa State Hospital in California. Dr. Kim is now Senior Psychiatrist at Parole Outpatient Clinic in Sacramento, California. Recently he joined the National Research Center on Asian-American Mental Health at the University of California, Davis. He is also Associate Clinical Professor of Psychiatry at the UC Davis School of Medicine. He is a Charter Fellow and a former board member of the Pacific Rim College of Psychiatrists, and Psychiatric Associate of the American Academy of Psychoanalysis. An original charter member of the APA Task Force on Asian-American Psychiatrists, Dr. Kim was the founding President of the Association of Korean-American Psychiatrists. He has authored 37 professional articles and 5 chapters, the majority of which are related to the subject of mental health of Korean-American immigrants and Korean-American children.

The KUN-PO SOO AWARD was established in 1987 to recognize significant contributions toward understanding the impact and import of Asian cultural heritage in areas relevant to psychiatry. The award also seeks to encourage scholarship and research in culture-specific mental health issues and treatment needs of Asian populations and to stimulate scientific exchange on transcultural issues.

Strengthening Psychiatry's Dedication and Commitment to:
Compassionate Care • Educational Excellence • Creative Research
San Diego 1997
American Psychiatric Association
Annual Meeting • May 17-22, 1997
San Diego, California

March 2010

3. C.V. of Grace Sangok Kim

Grace Sangok Kim

1781 Sunningdale Rd. #48
Seal Beach CA 90740
562-431-3039 graceokkimkim@aol.com
Ethnicity: Asian American; US Citizen; Marital status: married

Following retirement from their respective professional careers, Dr. and Mrs. Kim relocated themselves to a retirement community, Seal Beach Leisure World.Seal Beach, CA from Northern California, Davis, a small college town of UC Davis where she and her family lived in the same house for 36 years.

They moved to Southern CA, so that they can be nearby some of their family members, relatives, many old friends, as well as her girls' high school alumni friends and so many alumni of Seoul National University in Korea where Grace went to Teachers College while Luke went to SNU Medical School.

Education:

BA in education, Seoul National University, Seoul, Korea

MA in education and counseling, California Poly State University, San Luis Obispo, CA

30 unit graduate credits in counseling and health education after MA degree, mostly at UC Davis

Teaching Credentials:

State of California Standard Designated Teaching
Credential for vocational trade and technical field
General Teaching Credential, Elementary (K-8)
Standard Teaching Credential, Secondary (7-12)

Professional Experience:

1972-1996: Certificated Teacher, Davis Senior High School, Davis, CA (human development, human sexuality, health education, alcohol and drug abuse, family life and personal growth)

1982-1984: Instructor, Summer Bilingual/Bicultural institute, California State University Sacramento

1971-1973: Lecturer, University of California Davis Extension Division (Course in Early childhood education and parenting)

1970-1971: Head teacher, Yolo county Head Start Child Study Center

Professional and Community Activities (partial list):

1972-1974: Program director, National Association of Education of Young Children, Sacramento Chapter

1975: President, Committee for Early Childhood Needs, Davis, CA

1975: Consultant, Asian American Bilingual Resource Development Center, Berkeley, CA

1976-1977: Chair, Ethnic Concerns Committee, Synod of the Pacific, Presbyterian Church (USA)

1977-1982: Chair, Advisory Board, Crisis Counseling for Asian Wives of US Servicemen, Sacramento Presbytery, Presbyterian Church (USA)

1978-1983: Vice-chair, National Legal Defense Committee for Chol Soo Lee

1982-1983: Principal, Korean Language and Culture School of Sacramento, CA

1984-2006: Charter member, Davis Asians for Racial Equality (DARE)

1990: Member, Superintendent's Taskforce on Racial Climate Assessment, Davis Joint Unified School District, Davis, CA

1987-1991: Member, National Taskforce on Human Sexuality, Presbyterian Church (USA)

1992-1994: Member, Multicultural Curriculum and Instruction Committee, Davis Joint Unified School District

1996-1998: Vice-president, Korean American Community Association of Greater Sacramento

1997-2006: Member, Board of Directors, Pacific Rim Street Fest (Asian Pacific Rim Foundation), Old Sacramento

1997-1999:   Community advisor, Cal Expo
1996-2006:   Member, Asian Pacific American Community Advisory
                Board, KCRA (NBC) Channel 3 TV
1998-2006:   Instructor, officer training on cultural competency on
                Asian Americans, Davis Police department, Davis, CA
1998-2000:   Member, Asian Pacific Islander Community Advisory Council
                to Delaine Eastin, State Superintendent of Public Instruction
1998-2000:   President, Korean American Community Association of
                Greater Sacramento
1997-2008:   Board member, Korean American Coalition Sacramento
                Chapter Vice-chair, KAC National Board (current)
1998-2006:   Advisor, Korean American Adoptee and Adoptive Families
                National Network (KAAN)
1999-2006:   Member of the Executive Board, CAPITAL
2000-2006:   Member, Board of Directors, California Unity Council (a
                project for a $30 million new museum of multi-ethnic and
                multi-cultural history in California)
1972-2006:   Conducted numerous training workshops in communi-
                cations skills, parenting, racial relations and health
                education in API communities
2000-2003:   Elder, session member, Davis (Presbyterian) Community
                Church, Davis, CA
2000-2006:   Member, General Assembly Nominating Committee of
                Presbyterian Church (USA)
2006-2010:   Founder, Seal Beach Leisure World Multi-Cultural Annual
                Festival
2007-present: Organizer and Founder, Leisure World Korean American
                Choral Society
2009-2010:   Chair, Seal Beach Leisure World Community Church
                Personnel Committee

Awards and Certificates:

7/84:   Certificate of Appreciation by Korean American College
                Students National Leadership Conference, Los Angeles
5/85:   Community Service Award by the Christian Federation of
                Korean American Women in USA
6/89:   Outstanding Teacher Award by Davis Senior High School
                PTA

11/90:	Certificate of Outstanding Services by Board of Education, Davis Joint Unified School District.
4/91:	Certificate of Achievement ("for recognition of your numerous contributions in the area of human relations and cultural diversity") by Board of Education, Davis Joint Unified School District
1/92:	Certificate of Recognition ("in recognition of significant contribution to California public school") by Capitol Service Center Council, California Teachers Association
4/95:	Human Relations Award by City of Davis, CA
2/99:	Community Service Award by The Asian Bar Association of Sacramento
3/00:	Outstanding Contributions Award by UC Davis Asian American Studies
3/02:	Certificate of Outstanding Achievement by the Friends of Korea and Korean Adoptee and Adoptive Family Network (KAAN)
1/03:	Recipient of the Republic of Korea Presidential medal, "Dong Baek Jang" (second highest medal awarded to Korean civilians by President)
3/04:	Martin Luther King, Jr., Community Advocacy Award of Davis Community Coalition

Publications:

5. Editor/Project director., Korean Kaleidoscope: Oral Histories of Early Korean Pioneers in USA: 1903-1905, published by Sierra Mission Area, United Presbyterian Church, USA, 1982

6. "It's Okay To Say No," a chapter in Asian Presbyterian Women's Study Guide, published by United Presbyterian Church, USA, 1982

7. Editor, Inter-racial Marriage: Annotated Bibliography, published by Crisis Counseling Project for Asian Born Wives of US Servicemen, United Presbyterian Church, USA, 1983

8. "Women's Role in Presbyterian Church," a chapter in Presbyterian Resource Book. Published by Presbyterian Church, USA, 1984

9. "How To Tell Stories," a chapter in Teachers' Guide, United Methodist Church, USA, 1984

10. "A Plaza for Dialogue," a book published by Young Hak Press, Seoul, Korea, 1988. This is a collection of Weekly Column "Dear Grace" in Korean language newspapers

11. Weekly column "Dear Grace" from 1983 to 1989, in the Korea Times Los Angeles, USA, The column is similar to Dear Abby's questions and answer column.

12. Monthly article, "Dear Grace" in Korean People, a magazine in USA, 1986-1988

13. "Korean Immigrants and their children," published by Many Cultures Publishing, New Faces of Liberty, A Zellerbach Family Fund Project, 1994

14. "Asian North American Immigrants and Youth: Parenting and Growing up in a Cultural Gap," a chapter in *People on the Way,* edited by David Ng, Judson Press, Valley Forge, 1996

15. "Asian North American Youth: A ministry of Self-identity and Pastoral Care," a chapter in *People on the Way*, edited by David Ng, Judson Press, Valley, 1996

16. "One More Hurdle," a chapter in *Called Out With: Stories of Solidarity*, edited by S. Thorson-Smith, J.W. van Wijk-Bos, N. Pott, & W.P. Thompson, published by Westminster John Knox Press, Louisville, KY, 1997

17. Associate editor, CURRENTS, Asian American Community Newspaper of the Greater Sacramento area, from 6/1996 to present

18. Numerous articles in the Korea Times and Central Korean Daily "History of Korean Immigrants in the Sacramento Area" (in Korean) a chapter in book" History of Korean Immigration of Northern California" published by KA Immigration Centennial Committee, San Francisco, July, 2004

4. Samples of my father Kwon Zik Kim's memoir note, writings and drawings for his grandchildren

備 忘 錄

西紀 1902年陰12月1日 / 檀紀4235年陽1903年1月10日	朝鮮平安北道義州郡加山面都苓洞二統七 에서 出生하다 (當時父26세 母27세)
1909年(8세)	諺文敎를 父親의 指導로 믿기 始作하고 當未曾習어 나니다
1909~1911年11月	書堂에 通學하다
1911年12月6日(10세)	義州郡水鎭面松兆洞三統九戸로 全家族이 移舍하고 父親은 商業을 經營하다
1912.1 (11세)	水鎭面水口洞新在私立培新學校尋常科第二學年에 編入하다
1912.8.2	母親이 魏大模宣敎師에게 洗禮를 받다
1915.3	培新學校尋常科(4年制)優等卒業
".4	今校高等科第一學年入學
1916.12.3 (16세)	本人이 魏大模牧師에게 洗禮를 받다
1917.12	家族이 中國寬甸縣安子灘로 移舍하다 나는 催錦巖妹夫宅에서 通學하다
1919.2	培新學校高等科(四年制)卒業 (18세)
1919.3.1	義州農業學校入學試驗次義州邑妹夫金善瑛氏宅(운데우금柿골)에 갔다가 三一獨立萬歲運動에參 作되어 入學을 中止하다
1919.4	滿洲安子灘에 있는 우리집으로 돌아가다 寬甸縣安子灘獨立團安子灘事務所에서 臨時 書記視務하다(朴總務室)
1920.2	本國義州郡水鎭面大水洞230番地로 全家族移舍
1920.2~1921.3	水鎭面卧龍洞私塾(金仁瑗兄宅)에서 勤務
1921.4~1922.3	私立培新學校臨時教員視務
1921夏	義州公立普通學校夏期教員講習修了
1922.4	平壤崇實中學校第二學年編入 (家庭敎養20円)
1924.1.20	新義州緝砂町三丁目三一二로 移舍하다

Following life lessons and drawings are given by my father Kwon Zik Kim to his grandchildren

The life philosophy of my father Kwon Zik Kim:

- Be a person of beneficence (of help) to others, never be a burden to others.
- Be an independent person, and do not be a person who depends on others.
- Live a simple, honest, humble and economical life.
- Show examples by deed, and not by words.
- Truth, honesty and moral/ethical right and wrong are straightforward and clear, not buts, ifs and wishy-washy.
- Life is a continuing education. Cultivate and chart your life with learning, wisdom, faith and solid life philosophy. Try your best in whatever you do, but certain things may not work out the way you wished. It is important to accept the concept of your fate and destiny, and do not resent, lament or moan about your limitations, unfortunate circumstances or failures. God has a plan for you which you may not know fully sometimes. But trust, accept and obey His plan for you.

To: David and Danny and your children.

This is some of my life story and I hope you will get to know some thing about your Korean grandpa by reading this someday.

Kwon Zik Kim

Sept. 1976

The invention of Korea

① the print

Korean is the first of printing art.

② Korean porcelain

Now we can't make such good Korean porcelain

③ Korean letter
The King of Sejong had invented Korean letter as following

ㄱ ㄴ ㄷ ㄹ ㅁ ㅂ ㅅ ㅇ ㅈ ㅊ
ㅋ ㅌ ㅍ ㅎ
ㅏ ㅑ ㅓ ㅕ ㅗ ㅛ ㅜ ㅠ ㅡ ㅣ

16

You are american citizen. therefor you ought to perform american duty. Otherwise you are Korean american. You have Korean blood. Therefor you should love Korea. Take an interest in the accidents of Korea.

Sympathize the miserable people and help some thing you can. Give any convenience to the residents and the students studying abroad from Korea. I hope you should learn Korean language and the letter.

6

My grandson David,

You must build up your character.

The character is that fulfil three conditions following.

    ① Knowledge

    ② Virtue

    ③ Sports

① Sports is not first, the first is learning. Man must know science. It is not easy to be a doctor. Study hard, endure all distresses and then you should be successful.

② Obey your parents commandments and treat all men kindly, become a good man.

③ (A sound mind in a sound body) Move and train your body for health and strong.

           From   Kwon Zik Kim

敎育 (교육) **Education**

(一) 知 (지식)   **Knowledge**

(二) 德 (도덕)   **Virtue**

(三) 體 (체육)   **Health**

Grandfather explaining Korea by drawing maps for his grandchildren

(烏江洞) (古守翔面) (古館面) (加山面陪羽) (水頸面) (新義川)

弘倜 — 元澤 — 利云 — 仁 鍊 — 永浩 — 權 稷

金權稷 — 金益昌 ┬ 金聖喆 David ┐ Tessa
                       │   Julie   } Jasison
Kwon Zik Kim   │
           Luke Ik Chang Kim └ 金聖宇 Danny ┐ Jeffery
              Grace Kim   Janet   } Luke

(慶川)金仁鍊 —(慶川)金永浩 —(〃)金權稷 —(〃)金益昌
(安東)張炳鍊 —(大邱)金永和 ┬(新安)朱雲鳳 — 田常王
                        └(坡平)金英子

1978.

1958. 6. 23 現在
(55세)

5. Korea and Korean People

(This article is based on the edited copy from my chapter "Psychiatric Care of Korean Americans" in *Culture, Ethnicity and Mental Illness* edited by Albert Craw, American Psychiatric Press, Inc. Washington, DC, 1993, Pp 347-375)

Korean Americans are one of the fastest growing ethnic populations in the United States. The great majority of Korean Americans are immigrants who have arrived since 1965 after the ceasefire of the Korean War. In 1970, there were about 70,000 Korean Americans living in the United States; by 1980, the census registered 357,393. According to the 1990 U.S. Census (U.S. Bureau of the Census 1991), the count is now about 800,000. The recent 2000 U.S. Census indicated that the count of Koreans and Korean Americans was 1,076,872.

The Koreans are an ancient and relatively homogeneous people with a unique history, culture, and language distinct from both the Chinese and the Japanese. The founding of the first Korean states dates back to 2333 B.C., beginning with legendary Tang-gun.

Korea is a peninsula spanning 86,000 square miles, roughly the size of Minnesota. It is strategically located in the heart of northeast Asia, surrounded by the People's Republic of China, Japan, and the Russian Republic of the Commonwealth. All three nations have long been interested in dominating Korea and using the Korean peninsula as a bridge through which to invade neighboring countries. Korea's national history has been the story of its struggle to maintain independence from such external interference.

In the twentieth century alone, Korea was occupied by the Japanese from 1910 to 1945. After the end of World War II, the United States and the then-Soviet Union divided Korea into North and South Korea. The Korean War (1950-1953) erupted in the context of a Cold War struggle between the superpower camps. Unfortunately, Korea still remains divided, despite recent efforts to begin a dialogue toward unification of North and South Korea. Many Korean families are still separated because of this division.

Korea's geography as a natural bridge between the Asian mainland and Japan not only invited military attack over the centuries, but also provided a cultural link between China and Japan. Confucianism and

Buddhism, along with other aspects of art and culture, were introduced to Japan through Korea. However, Koreans have been able to maintain their own unique cultural identity in terms of language, art, customs, and beliefs.

[5 A] The Contemporary Collective Experience of Koreans: Historically, Koreans have experienced great strife and hardships and thus, Koreans are called people of *Haan* (a Korean word—feelings of everlasting woe (KW. Lee), a form of victimization syndrome)(further discussion is referred to the full text of Korean Ethos in the Appendix). In this century alone, Korea has been under colonial rule or divided by foreign hegemony for more than 80 years. After the division of Korea at the end of World War II, several million Koreans escaped from the Communist-dominated North to South Korea. During the Korean War alone, Korea had more than 3 million military and civilian casualties.

Koreans have dealt with such social turmoil through various means. Confucian teaching has been a fundamental and traditional force in Korean culture, although in recent decades Christianity has gained a strong influence. Self-reliance, self-discipline, and a strong work ethic are emphasized, and education and academic achievement arc considered important steps in achieving success and social distinction (Yu and Kim 1983). In Korean society, the family is the dominant social unit, and respect for parents, elders and teachers is inculcated in Korean young people.

Studying the lives of recent Korean immigrants in the United States, researchers found that the characteristic values and culture of Koreans tend to give them a head start in American life. However, Korean immigrants in the United States, like other immigrants, have experienced personal and institutional racial discrimination. Moreover, Korean immigrants are often regarded as the minority of minorities among Asian Americans. Because of their comparatively brief immigration history, Korean American immigrants have much less political and community clout than, for example, Japanese Americans and Chinese Americans have in some locales. In spite of their hard and determined work to establish themselves as American citizens, Koreans have been the object of hate crimes and interethnic conflict. This kind of difficulty is reflected in the tension in some neighborhoods between Korean immigrants and African Americans. This was amply demonstrated in the May 1992 Los Angeles riot, when much of Koreatown was destroyed.

[5 B] The History of Korean Immigration to the United States: In terms of their relationship with the West, Korea had remained the "Hermit Kingdom" until 1882 when Korea and the United States signed a treaty. Following the treaty, a team of Korean diplomatic envoys visited the United States in 1883 and 1884, and soon afterward, the first Korean legation was established in Washington, DC.

[5 C] The First Wave: Before 1903, about 50 Korean students, political exiles, and merchants had arrived individually on American shores. The first great wave of Korean immigration to America occurred from 1903 to 1905. By 1905, a total of 7,226 Korean immigrants (6,048 men, 637 women, 541 children) had reached Hawaii in 65 different ships. Another 1,033 Koreans immigrated to Mexico. The majority of immigrants who came from Korean port cities were young bachelors between the ages of 20 and 30 and were largely un-educated. They were recruited as laborers in sugar plantations in Hawaii. Because of the unbalanced gender ratio (10 men to every woman), frequent exchanges of photographs between prospective grooms in Hawaii and brides in Korea took place so that marriages could be arranged. As a result, 1,100 picture brides arrived from 1910 to 1924. Even so, many early male Korean immigrants (about 3,000) spent the rest of their lives as bachelors.

Plantation life for these early immigrants was very hard because of segregation, low wages, extremely strenuous work, as well as language and cultural barriers. They endured this harsh life with hopes of returning to Korea someday. However, when Korea was occupied by Japan in 1910, they had no country to return to.

Based on our own Oral History Project on early immigrants in Hawaii[1], we found out that the picture brides were generally much better educated than their husbands were. In spite of discriminations and hardship they faced, the picture bride wives were planning their lives with a very active, forward looking and entrepreneurial spirit and orientation. Thus, they encouraged their husbands, instead of being stuck in hard labor in sugar plantations, to explore and seek self-employed jobs or business, such

---

[1]   Korea Kaleidoscope: Oral Histories, Vol. one. Early Korean Pioneers in UA: 1903-1905, Published by Korean Oral History Project, Davis, CA. 1982

as, barbershop, small inn or motel, neighborhood stores, after receiving necessary trainings. Indeed they were the backbone of their families and the Korean American communities. They started Korean language schools for their children, organized patriotic societies, and sacrificed their own scarce funds to support the Korean Independence movements. The well-known community leader in Hawaii at that time was Syngman Rhee, who later established the Korean government-in-exile in Shanghai; he was elected as the first president of the Republic of Korea in 1948.

Subsequent to their initial migration to Hawaii, some early Korean immigrants moved to the U.S. mainland. The 1930 U.S. census showed fewer than 2000 Koreans on the mainland, most of them based in California. They were subjected to severe racial discrimination, and they were described as the "minority of minorities." Their life was a courageous, lonesome struggle in a hostile environment. Because the early Korean immigrants placed a high value on education, their children and grandchildren were encouraged to attain high levels of education, and many of them became successful professionals in the mainstream society.

[5 D] The Second Wave:
The second wave of Korean immigrants arrived in the United States between 1951 and 1964. This was a heterogeneous group: Korean wives of U.S. servicemen, war orphans, and students. A survey indicates that 37,063 Korean wives of U.S. servicemen arrived in the United States from 1950 to 1977. These Korean wives of U.S. servicemen were doubly marginal, both in the American society and in the Korean immigrant community. They suffered from culture shock, lack of education, isolation, poor communication in the family, a high divorce rate, and general alienation. There were some happy marriages, but physical abuse and mental health problems characterized many relationships, which often ended in divorce.

Much less is known about Korean War orphans. Early surveys indicated "a successful," positive adjustment and integration of the KA adoptees into the American family and society. However, a later study showed that the adopted children encountered some racial problems as they became older because of their Asian physical appearance. The adoptees were seen as Asian, yet they were almost totally cut off from other Asian ethnics and from Korean culture. Having to live with a dual identity but, for the most part, without ethnic support, they may have had psychological problems as they grew older.

The last group in the second wave of immigrants consisted of students who came to the United States to study at universities. About 6,000 came between 1945 and 1965. Although the data available for later years overlap with this data set, another survey showed that between 1953 and 1980, a total of 15,147 Korean students left for the United States with student visas. In addition, there were at least 2,000-3,000 Korean physicians who were in training as interns and residents in American medical centers during this period. Although no accurate data are available, the majority of these students and physicians remained in the United States and succeeded in professional careers. Those who returned to Korea became leaders in their fields.

[5 E] The Third Wave: The third large wave of Korean immigration was spearheaded by the Immigration and Naturalization Act of 1965, which raised the ceiling for the immigration quota among Asian countries. As a result, Koreans have become one of the most rapidly growing immigrant populations in the United States. This group of Korean newcomers is very different in composition from the previous immigrants. Most of the latest immigrants consisted of young families with a mean adult age of 27.3 and an average household size of 3.8. The immigrants come from urban, middle-class backgrounds, and half of them are college graduates. About 50% of them held professional, technical, or managerial jobs in Korea. However, fewer than one-third of these professionals have found comparable jobs after their arrival in the United States. This downward mobility has resulted in an increase in the number of Korean owners of small businesses, such as dry cleaning stores, small groceries, fast food restaurants, and other blue-collar or nonprofessional occupations.

During the period from 1966 to 1979, some 13,000 Korean medical doctors, dentists, nurses, and pharmacists entered the United States.

Korean immigrants are evenly dispersed throughout the country, although they are more heavily concentrated in large urban areas such as Los Angeles, New York, Chicago, Baltimore, and Washington, DC. About half of them own homes in suburban areas.

Although only 25% of the population in Korea is Christian, 60%-70% of the new U.S. immigrants from Korea attend Korean ethnic Christian churches. There are more than 2,000 Korean churches in the United States. The rapid increase in the number of these Korean ethnic churches is quite remarkable. This phenomenon of attending ethnic Christian churches in a high proportion has not been found among other ethnic groups. Many

Korean immigrants who were non Christian in Korea may have been attracted to these Korean ethnic churches because they feel isolated and the ethnic church provides social and psychological support in addition to religious functions. Korean Christian churches seem to play the role of extended family to the otherwise isolated nuclear families, and they contribute an important function to social networking and community building among Korean immigrants.

(Further Revised on 4/28/11)

6. KOREAN ETHOS

Luke I. Kim, M.D., Ph.D.
University of California Davis School of Medicine

2010 January revised version of the paper of
the journal of KAMA Volume 2, Number 1, 1996

If we were to describe the predominant ethos of Americans—those values which influence their social, political and personal life—we would name: individual freedom, independence, self-reliance, privacy and fun. Western psychology has been more interested in the individual person, in individual psychology, ego structure and what is happening in the person's psyche than in the community.

In the traditional Asian feudal and/or agrarian village society, people lived together and worked together mostly in a group setting or in close proximity to each other. Their economic, social and emotional lives were tied to each other. In such an environment, allegiance to each other is important. The interest of the group takes priority over the interest of the individual member (SC Choi, UC kim, SH Choi, 1993). There is a need for emotional bonding to each other for mutual help and support. They need to find ways to live together in harmony. The ideology of freedom, independence, individuality and privacy is not developed. An individual did not exist alone or independently, but existed mainly in close relations with his/her extended family and collective network. With this orientation, it was difficult to define one's identity without reference to the collective identity to which an individual belonged. They were more conscious of group identity than of personal identity (JH Cha, 1994). Thus Asian psychological interest has been more focused on the psychology of human relations than in the psychology of the individual. It was further reinforced by the Confucian teachings which were primarily concerned with human relations.

Lebra describes Japanese psyche as consisting of "Ego" (*Jibun*, じ-ぶん, 自分) and social object, namely, "Alter" (*Hito*, ひと, 人, another human being), with the two influencing each other (T. Lebra. 1976). Indian culture emphasizes family ego more than individual ego. Ego is characterized as "porous" with the individual ego and the family ego interacting with each other.

This "porous ego" would be regarded as undesirable or pathological by Western psychology which stresses the importance of the individual ego being protected by firm and strong ego boundaries. However, in the American society, people are increasingly fearful and distrustful of each other, and the institution of marriage, family values, and sense of community are declining. This declining tendency may be attributed, at least partially, to the predominant ideology of individualism.

In recent years, it has been recognized that there is a danger in dichotomizing cultures into individualism and collectivism in a black and white manner. It not only clouds our understanding of the otherwise very complex interactions of the two orientations, but also it inevitably leads to our making good/bad comparisons. Attempts have been made to develop a conceptual model of coexistence of individualism and collectivism, and to avoid the distorted dichotomy of either individualism or collectivism (D Sinha & RC Tripathi, 1994). I agree with above statement and feel important that every effort should be made to integrate individualism and collectivism.

In this article, I will attempt to describe some of the more important Korean ethos which have greatly influenced Koreans and their social and interpersonal behavior, especially in the "old days." They are: *Jeong* (정, 情), *Haan* (한, 恨), *O-gi* (오기, 傲氣), *Che-myun* (체면, 體面), *Noonchi* (눈치), *Palja* (팔자, 八字), and *Muht* (멋). However, with rapid westernization, industrialization, and urbanization, Korean/Asian societies are going through phenomenal changes in their social structure, values and interpersonal relations. People are becoming more individualistic, and less collectivistic than 40 or 50 years ago. This coincides with the beginning of Westernization in Asian countries following the end of World War II. Korean/Asian people are now in a confused transitional state in terms of knowing where they are going. Furthermore, the ideology of individualism with emphasis on materialistic success is taking a strong hold in Asian continents. Therefore, the validity of the "traditional" Korean ethos described below is weakening in the present day.

The Korean ethos concept of *Jeong* is disappearing, although we can still observe that *Che-myun* 체면 (face-saving) and *Muht* 멋 (refinement/elegance/charm) remain strong. In order to understand Koreans' psyche and their social behavior, it is important to know and understand the Korean ethos (L Kim, 1990).

Most young second generation Korean Americans in the United States probably have never heard about the word *Jeong* 정 情. They might have experienced *jeong* relations among family members, especially parental love, but they may not have the slightest idea what *jeong* is. It is my hope that an article, like this, will document and let the younger generations know how their older immigrant parents and grandparents lived in "the old days." It would be also helpful to non-Korean mental health professionals to have a knowledge of the Korean ethos in order to understand Korean immigrant clients better in a therapy setting.

JEONG, 정, 情

There is no word in the Korean vocabulary more endearing and evocative than the word *Jeong*. *Jeong* refers to a special interpersonal bond of trust and closeness. There is no English equivalent. *Jeong* encompasses the meaning of a wide range of English terms: feeling, empathy, affection, closeness, tenderness, pathos, compassion, sentiment, trust, bonding and love.

Jeong strengthens the bonding of the relationship between two persons. It is a special affection toward a person. It is not a sexualized or erotic love. Koreans considers *jeong* an essential element in human life, promoting the depth and richness of personal relations. With *jeong*, relationships are deeper and longer lasting. In times of social upheaval, calamity, and unrest, *jeong* is the only binding and stabilizing force in human relationships. Without *jeong*, life would be emotionally barren, and we would feel isolated and disconnected from others. *Jeong* is more than kindness or liking another. *Jeong* brings about the "special" feelings in relationships: togetherness, sharing, bonding, and we-feeling, *Woo-ri* (우리). *Jeong* is what makes us say "we" rather than "I," and "ours" rather than "mine." (Kim, 1994).

The word, *jeong*, is usually combined with another word that modifies the nuances of meaning and defines the relationship. *Mo-Jeong* (모정, 母

情) (*Mo* = mother), is *Jeong* bonding between a mother and child. *Jeong* between two friends or among friends is "*Woo-Jeong* (우정, 友情) (*Woo* = friend)." *Ae-Jeong* (애정, 愛精) (*Ae* = love) is lovers' *jeong; In-Jeong* (인정, 人情) (*In* = human) is human sympathy with universal compassion. *Shim-Jeong* (심정, 心精) (*Shim* = heart) is "*jeong* in the heart." It is the emotions we feel about another person in our heart. *Jeong* relationship between teacher and student is that of an enduring mentorship, not merely a relationship where the teacher has the duty to transmit knowledge to the student. The teacher's role in Korea is, more or less, *Jeong*-related mentorship guiding the student's life and future as a coach.

Chinese, Japanese and Koreans share the general concept of *jeong*, but each country appears to give a somewhat different emphasis in their concepts. The Chinese emphasize the aspect of loyalty and reciprocity in relationships, while the Japanese equivalent "*Jyo.*" tends to emphasize sentimental feelings. "*Jyo ni moroi* (じょう にもろい)" means that one is weak and vulnerable through sentimentality. *Ki-ri* (ぎり) (responsibility and royalty) (기리, 義理) is considered the most important ethos among Japanese. Koreans, however, give more importance to the aspect of *Jeong* focusing on the development of interpersonal bonding and emotional attachment between two individuals.

Jeong develops not only in horizontal relations such as friendship, but also in vertical relationships, such those between parent and child, or between teacher and student. "*Woo-jeong* (友情)", *jeong* of two friends, connotes more than an ordinary friendship. Of course, there are different levels of "*Woo-jeong*," but typically, the friendship is deeper and longer lasting than one between ordinary friends. There is a special quality of having shared fate together, such as the mutual bond of camaraderie and brotherhood such as one that develops between two soldiers in war time who fought together in the frontline trenches, and shared life and death experiences. *Jeong* can develop among classmates, high school or college alumni friends who share a faith or common interest, or among professional colleagues. The concept of "soul mate" perhaps comes close to capturing the essence of a friendship with deep *jeong*.

Jeong is not erotic and not sexualized. There is no implication of a homosexual relationship. The only erotic *jeong* is "*Ae-jeong* (愛情, love-*jeong*)," the *jeong* between ; husband and wife, or between two lovers, although some would say that erotic *jeong* is also present between a mother and her baby.

Although *jeong* can develop mutually among a group of people, such as alumni, through group identification. It is usually cultivated in a dyadic situation where there has been a give-and-take interaction between the two people. *Jeong* is usually reciprocated, but it can be unilateral. *Jeong* is not experienced instantly, but grows over time. It is not "love at first sight." It needs a certain period of "incubation" so that the *jeong* bonding can occur. *Jeong* is like water coming up slowly and gently seeping through sand on the beach. It is not a gush of water. The process occurs more naturally and less intentionally than in love.

JEONG **AND LOVE:** The concept of love has been richly dealt with in the history of Western culture and religions. The Western concept of love includes a variety of types: divine love (Agape), erotic love, maternal love, brotherly/sisterly love, platonic love, altruistic love, to name a few. But *jeong* does not fit into any one of these categories. *Jeong* is the common denominator within all of these types of love. One may say that "love" itself is also the common denominator. "Love" is a beautiful and powerful English word, but unfortunately the word has been overused, abused, commercialized, and sexualized to the degree that the word "love" had lost its clarity, beauty, meaning and power. *Jeong* can be love in the Western sense, but there are important differences in the nuance and quality. I would characterize those differences as follows:

LOVE (Western)
- more direct in expression

- more physical, behavioral

- more action-oriented

- active, positive, forward, outward

- more need/desire-related more intentional, volitional

- tends to be possessive

- more contractual

- differentiated with boundary—separated self

- happiness, joy

JEONG (Asian)
- more indirect in emotional expression

- more affective, attitudinal

- more relational

- more inward, yearning for, waiting and thinking

- warm, caring, and enduring

- more survival—and connection-related

- more naturally developing

- It is not the love at first sight, but requires incubation period for bonding to occur before one can love

- could be passive/aggressive

- tends to be protective

- more unconditional

- less differentiated, and more fused more

- "good earth-mother" archetype

- love

We can also contrast the imagery of "erotic" love with that of *Jeong*. Erotic love can be described as hot, fiery, dynamic, intense, mercurial, pleasurable, unpredictable, and powerful. The imagery of *Jeong*, on the other hand, is: quiet, gentle, nurturing, caring, giving, trusting, loyal, considerate, devoted, dependable, and sacrificial (*Wee hae joon da*).

Reflecting on the above lists of adjectives, I feel that the *jeong* concept has more feminine quality of love, similar to the "self-in-relation" theory of the feminine psychology which emphasizes caring, connectedness and nurturing relations in love (Baker-Miller 1976, Gilligan 1982, Prozan 1992).

The ideal prototype of *jeong* would be "*Mo-jeong*," meaning maternal love: a good earth—mother type of embracing, unconditionally accepting, and bonding.

There is a Korean expression, "*go woon jeong* (고운 정), *mi woon jeong* (미운 정)," meaning "a beautiful *jeong* and hateful *jeong*." The idea is that once *jeong* is established between the two persons, the *jeong* bond and trust is unbreakable, even if the relationship goes through hateful and turbulent periods. The Buddhist implication is that the two are bonded together affectively forever by fate, whether they like it or not.

JEONG AND PSYCHOANALYTIC INSIGHT:

Does contemporary psychoanalytic thinking offer any insight or clue to help us understand the role of *jeong* in our lives?

In his self-psychology, Kohut placed great importance on the role of empathy in the healthy development of the self (H Kohut, 1977). He stated that the empathic responses which emanate from parental figures first, and subsequently from other people, play a decisive role in building substance of the nuclear self. These "others" are called "self objects," because they function as nourishing elements of the self. Kohut emphasized that a person needs to experience at every stage of life emphatic and affirmative responses from people, or "self objects." From this core experience emerge the sense of substance and continuity of one's self through time.

Freud viewed the essence of human nature as the "guilty person," wrestling between the id and the superego, whereas Kohut described human nature as a "tragic person," who is in search of empathic relationships in the restoration of self suffering from inner emptiness, isolation and unfulfillment. I feel that the unique characteristics of *jeong* as empathic interpersonal relationships would be a valuable ingredient in affirming and encouraging the development and maintenance of a sense of self.

I feel that Winnicott's concept of "holding environment" helps us understand how it is important and essential to have a stable, holding environment for healthy emotional growth (DW Winnicott, 1965, 1986b). Again it is compatible with the idea of emotionally nurturing environment supported by the positive acceptance and affirming relationships of *jeong*.

Among the psychologists, there has been much interest in the concept of attachment that is necessary between the mother and infant for healthy child development. Also during the adult life, supportive interpersonal relationship in the form of attachment phenomenal is important for the continuous growth of the individual's healthy life.I have already touched on the differences or contrast between love and *jeong* in the table.

Jeong appears to have a different affective quality than that of love. It seems that *Jeong* represents a more primordial and primitive ways of relating than love, almost similar to an affect of mother-infant union or "return-to-the-womb," a symbolic world of being more fused and less separated in the individuation-separation process. It has the quality of symbiotic interdependency. The concept of *jeong* corresponds with a "good earth-mother" type of love, as well as Jungian archetype. In contrast, the "western" love appears to be an affective experience of union in a developmentally more mature and individuated state (ES Park, 1995).

BOUNDARY ISSUE:Western psychiatrists or psychologists have raised boundary issues. They often raise a question that such *jeong* relationship in the family may contribute to developing "an enmeshed family" and "poor ego boundaries." It is true that, according to the Western point of view, most Korean families tend to be ammeshed with *jeong* relations, with the consequence of presumably "poor ego strength and ego boundaries" of individuals. The word "enmeshment" is a negative term, but it does not have to be from the Asian point of view. Asians feel that individual independence is a Western idea and maybe a desirable goal for Westerners, but for Asians, good "human relationships" are a desirable goal, and more important than individual independence. If individualism is pushed too hard, it may lead to a breakdown of marriage, family, and community. Each individual may exist for themselves without a sense of belonging and community, and is inclined to "do my own thing." Already there are too many lonely and isolated people in the US. A recent trend to return to family values in the American political debate is indicative of the awareness that emphasis on individual independence and freedom perhaps may have gone too far, and needs to be pulled back a little.

In the American way, people call a person by name (especially the first name), such as among siblings, sometimes even uncles or step-father. In the Asian way, a person is addressed or called by the nature of the relationship, i.e. younger or older brother, mother's son, or brother-in-law, etc.

The idea that due to family enmeshment ego boundaries are blurred and ego strength is weakened. This suggests that somehow there would be many more psychopathology and psychotic disorders in Korea or Asia than in the U.S. There are no data to support such a view.

In a Western society, people go to a professional counselor when they have a problem and need to talk with someone for help. In Korea and Asia, they are likely to go to someone they can trust for counseling and advice. The person they can trust is likely to be a person with whom they are *jeong*-bonded. In such a relation of trust, they would be able to talk and really open up to each other for intense sharing and understanding, as well as for mutual advice. It would be hard for Koreans to readily open up to a mental health professional who is a stranger, without developing some degree of *jeong* trust between the two. It will take time and will need a trusting, nurturing period of "incubation" to feel closer and develop *jeong* feeling. That is one of the reasons why professional counseling has not become well developed nor developed rapidly in Asian countries.

Some Western psychiatrists and psychologists are of the opinion that Koreans/Asians are not psychologically minded and are not suitable for psychodynamic psychotherapy. I disagree. Once a relation of *jeong* is developed with the therapist, psychological and emotional interactions would be very rich, intense, psychologically savvy and quick-minded. It would not be much different from the experience of transference and counter-transference (L. Kim, 1992).

THE NEGATIVE SIDE OF *JEONG*: While *jeong* makes it possible to enrich our life and environment with nurturing and meaningful personal relations, it does have a dark side with serious side effects. In its pure form, *jeong*, like love, may expect and demand the reciprocity of loyalty and trust. Therefore, if that loyalty is betrayed, it can be as hurtful and destructive as when love is betrayed.

As already mentioned above, boundary issues can be problematic. Westerners and Westernized Koreans may fear that their personal and private lives could be easily encroached upon, intruded or interfered with by *jeong* related people. This can be a source of conflict and tension. We need a balance between privacy and connectedness.

Another dark side of *jeong* is about the risk of developing in-group vs. out-group phenomena. It has the potential of leading people to protect each other within the circle of the in-group, and discriminating against outsiders (SW Lee & HN Lee, 1993). That was the way they used to survive and protect themselves against invaders in feudal/tribal villages and provinces in the past. Koreans are known for being very kind, helpful, hospitable and compassionate to members of their affiliates, but they may be lacking in these attributes toward strangers and outsiders.

Some criticize that Koreans are too survival-oriented, and that they are primarily concerned with their family members, their kids and friends. They say that Koreans are weak in social and community conscience, social justice, and public etiquette (KW Lee, 1995). Also regional distrust and biases still exist in Korea. In this regard, Koreans/Asian countries can learn lessons from the experiences of American society in its effort to promote social justice.

Related concern is that *jeong* relations can cloud one's rational objectivity in the process of decision-making, such as in business transactions, personnel selection, etc., resulting in a potential risk for nepotism and corruption. Mixing *jeong*-relations with official matters in public life has created problems in Asian countries. As citizens become more sophisticated and enlightened politically with strong public education and respect for law, there should be every effort to stop mixing public matters with private personal relations, especially, in the public and political arena.

The in-group vs. out-group phenomena have split community organizations, and have been damaging Korean-Americans' efforts to organize themselves effectively in a community-wide effort for political and social causes. That is because organizations are often influenced by personal relations centering around a strong group leader.

Finally, I feel that the unique Korean/Asian concept of *Jeong* can help us understand a new dimension of human emotions and interpersonal relationships, especially among Korean/Asians, that has thus far not been known to Western psychology. In spite of some side-effects, *Jeong*-relations are generally conducive to life-affirmation and emotional nurturing. *Jeong* is a fascinating concept in the Asian tradition that deserves further attention and study.

HAAN 한, 恨

Haan (恨) is the opposite of *jeong* (情). It is the Korean word which refers to suppressed anger, hate, despair, the holding of a grudge, or feelings of "everlasting woe" (KW Lee, 1995). Anger is likely to transform into *haan* feelings over time, when one cannot express anger and rage outwardly, and when one cannot, act out, revenge, forget, push away, get over with, resolve, dissolve or unknot the anger, especially in the old days when they did not have many options. Koreans so readily understand and deeply experience *haan* that it is a folk term used by common people.

The original Chinese character for *haan* has the meaning of "to get even with, to revenge." But when we look at how Koreans have used the word, we see that it takes on different meanings. The Korean use of the word emphasizes aspects of suppression of anger, indignation, and holding a grudge. The notion of getting even with is secondary. In English, the spelling of *Haan* has been Romanized. Frequently, it is spelled as Han, and it has also appeared in English article as Hahn and *Haan*. *Haan* has a long vowel sound, almost like sighing, which is why I prefer the spelling *Haan*. Also if spelled *Hahn* or *Han*, the word often gets confused with a surname *Hahn* or the *Han* dynasty of the Chinese.

The word *Haan* is often combined with a second word to express the different nuances of *haan* feeling. Examples are: *Haan-tan* (한탄, 恨嘆) which means "crying and lamenting *haan*"; *Hwoe-haan* (회한, 悔恨) which means "*haan* with remorse and regret", similar to the Japanese word *zan-nen* (ざん-ねん, 残念); *Won-haan* (원한, 怨恨), which is "revengeful *haan*"; *Jung-haan* (정한, 靜恨) which is a "*haan* of passive acceptance and resignation."

Korean scholars believe that *haan* is not simply a private emotion of a person who has suffered a lot; rather it is a pervasive "collective" emotional state among Koreans who historically have experienced an abundance of tragedies and pain in their lives. As a result of its geographic positioning (Korea is a bridge situated between China, Japan and Russia) Korea has been invaded and occupied frequently by surrounding military forces. Korea has even become a tributary nation to China and Japan. Under foreign military occupation, Korea—"the land of Morning Calm"—has been trampled, burned, and destroyed repeatedly.

Even in the twentieth century, Korea was occupied by Japan for 35 years until the end of World War II. Even after her liberation from Japan, Korea was divided into two Koreas, a tragic victim of superpower cold war strategy. Millions of North Koreans escaped from Communist North Korea to South Korea leaving behind family members, relatives and friends. To this day, they have not seem their loved ones in over 60 years ago. In addition, the Korean war erupted killing millions of people, including many American and UN soldiers. The Korean War ended some 60 years ago, but the political problems have not yet been solved. The tension between North and South Korea, and the threat of military action, are continuous. Some call the tragic division of Korea as a "modern day Korean *haan*" (SC Paik, 1993).

Each war, each political and social upheaval, brought about suffering, personal losses, and unbearable woe to Koreans. Few have been spared the loss, pain, and suffering. Most have fought and struggled for survival, and somehow managed to exist. Some even have thrived. But they harbor deep feelings of *haan*: suppressed anger, resentment, and underlying depression. They have suffered feelings of indignation at having been victimized unfairly. However, for their own survival, as well as to live in harmony with the teachings of Confucius, they have had to swallow and suppress their feelings.

The *haan* in the "collective subconscious psyche" of Korea is related to historical, political and social upheavals Korea has encountered for many centuries. But, in addition, there has been a great deal of personal misery, suffering and victimization in the domestic lives of Koreans. Traditionally, Korea had been a class-oriented society in which the ruling class, the "*Yangban* (양반, 兩班)" oppressed and abused the poor and the underclass, the "*Ssang-nom* (쌍놈)". Also in the traditional Confucian society, the status and role of the female is subservient to that of the male. As a result, women have to endure much hardship and injustice. The poor and powerless had no recourse to appeal the injustice. In order to tolerate it, they had to moderate their anger and indignation. Some scholars (KS Choi, 1991) speak of two different sources of *haan*: a *haan* derived from *kong-no* which means "anger over public matters," such as social and political injustice, and a *haan* derived from *sa-no*, "anger over personal matters," i.e. abuses by in-laws or husband.

FOUR PHASES OF *HAAN*:

Sang-Chin Choi (1993), a Korean psychologist, described the four experiential phases of *haan*. The first phase is experiencing rage, anger, hostility, hate, and desire for revenge for the injustice done to him to her. An example would be: a wife who had been cruelly treated and abused by her mother-in-law, especially in the old days when it was impossible to divorce. She realizes that she cannot do much in the way of retaliation and revenge toward her mother-in-law. Therefore, in the face of reality and the situation, she tries to, or has no choice but to try to, control and suppress her anger and rage. She would start reevaluating the situation, and begin to feel that perhaps it was her fault, at least, partially. This would help her dull the intensity of her anger. She begins to entertain some self-blame. This is the second phase. She would feel depressed and pessimistic.

The third phase is the period when she begins to dwell on the situation again, and starts questioning the rationale of her second phase thinking, namely, self-blame. "I am powerless. I do not have power nor position to get even with my mother-in-law. Is it my fault? Isn't it injustice? Why does this have to happen to me? Why me?" She begins to feel sad and resigned. This sadness phase may last a long time. This melancholic sentimentality could be expressed in a sublimated way. If she is talented, into singing, writing of diaries or poetry, and other art forms. It is usually about this phase of *haan* when Koreans discuss *haan*. The second phase is a transitory phase between the first and the third phase.

In the fourth phase, she begins to detach her *haan* feeling from herself by putting emotional distance and objectifying her *haan* experiences. She might talk about it as if it belonged to someone else.

She would describe it as a third person's experience. During this phase, she may be calmer, more silent, and lonely. Her *haan* feelings could even be transformed into trans-reality and transpersonal experiences. She may accept it as her fate.

HAAN AND SYMBOLISM:

Some call Korea a nation of *haan*, and a nation of suffering. A Korean psychiatrist stated that *haan* is "something that has been formed, accumulated, and precipitated on mass in the depth of Korean psyche over generations—it is deeply imprinted in the collective subconscious of the

Korean people" (Prince 1989). A well known poet, Ko-Un (고은, 高銀), expressed his view graphically: "Koreans are born from the womb of *haan*, grow up in the bosom of *haan*, and live with *haan*, then die, leaving *haan* behind."

When seen in this way, *haan* is a symbol, a sign-language of the Korean psyche and Korean history. *Haan* is the Korean version of victimization syndrome analogous to the Holocaust when used as a symbol by the Jewish people. Korean folklore, songs, poems, novels, dancing, art work, and autobiographical literature are full of *haan*-ridden stories where motive and themes are derived from *haan* experiences.

A *haan*—ridden person feels that he or she is an innocent victim, who suffers not because of one's own fault or mistake, but because of the fault or mistake of another. That someone else could be a bad master, an abusive husband, a cruel mother-in-law, a corrupt government, or an invading foreign power. Or it could be fate, nature, calamity or supernatural power. The common expression used to express *haan* feelings is: "*Uh-gul-ha-da*", which refers to feelings of indignation at the injustice done to him or to her.

A Korean theologian, Suk-mo Ahn (1992) takes the interpretation of *haan* one step further. For him, *haan* refers not only to pent-up emotion of anger and the holding of a grudge, but also carries the image of woundedness, the wrecked meaning of life, the fragmentation of self and the world, and most of all, a strong sense of "why me? and "why this to me?" It is almost akin to the experience of mourning.

HAAN (한, 恨) AND *HWA-BYUNG* (화병, 火病):

From a clinical point' of view, *haan* is considered as a causative factor in the development of a Korean culture-bound psychiatric syndrome called "*Hwa-byung*". *Hwa-byung* literally means "fire (*Hwa*, 화, 火) disease (*Byung*, 병, 病)" or "anger disease." The syndrome manifests in the mixture of clinical depression, anxiety and somatic symptoms characterized by the presence of a "lump" and pressure in the throat or chest (SH Lee.1977a). The syndrome is most common among women, especially married women who are beyond middle age and of low social class standing.

According to Sung Kil Min's survey (1986) of 100 *Hwa-byung* patient seen at the Yonsei University Hospital Outpatient Clinic, Seoul, Korea, the symptoms most frequently complained of were: oppressive and heavy feelings in the chest, a feeling of a mass in the chest or abdomen; a feeling of something hot pushing in the chest; a sensation of heat in the body; feelings of something boiling up, or burning inside. Other physical symptoms include: headaches, palpitation, indigestion, etc. Generally the patients complained of physical symptoms, but when they were asked about emotional symptoms, they frequently mentioned were: sadness, pessimistic view, loss of interest, temper, startling, nervousness, and even suicidal thoughts. Other emotions include: rage, hate, resentment, frustration, mortification, regret and shame.

Hwa-byung has been known in Korea as a folk medical term for a long time. Interestingly, Korean immigrant patients who were seen at clinics in Los Angeles manifested symptoms of *Hwa-byung*. It was Keh-Ming Lin (1983) of UCLA who first reported in an English language psychiatric journal citing 3 Korean *Hwa-byung* cases in 1983. Subsequently several research articles appeared in the American journals, which aroused an interest in the syndrome among mental health professionals (KY Pang, 1990).

Hwa-byung is now listed as one of culture-bound syndromes in the appendix of the Revised Diagnostic Manual (DSM IV) published by the American Psychiatric Association (1994). The DSM—IV edition describes *Hwa-byung* as: "A Korean folk syndrome literally translated into English as "anger syndrome" and attributed to the suppression of anger. The syndrome include insomnia, fatigue, panic, fear of impending doom, dysphonic affect, indigestion, anorexia, palpitation, generalized aches and pains, and a feeling of a mass in the epigastrium. There have been debates as to whether or not *Hwa-byung* is considered as a Korean culture-bound syndrome, or a clinical syndrome of "anger disease" that is more universal in nature, but is called differently in different ethnic cultures.

Of interest are the findings that most *Hwa-byung* patients were aware that the cause of *Hwa-byung* is psychogenic in nature. When they were asked what they thought caused the symptoms, most answered that the symptom stems from suppressed *Hwa* (anger and fire) for too long.

In the survey, when they were asked what kind of difficulties they thought were associated with their personal *Hwa*, their problems were multiple. 72% of them said they were having trouble with their spouses in the form of such things as extramarital affairs, alcoholism, and domestic violence. 6S% had in-law problems, and 35% felt their difficulties with their children could be attributed to *Hwa*. In addition, social factors were cited: 65% were related to poverty, 58% some kind of life hardship, and 32% unfair blame and criticism.

HAAN AND RELIGIONS:

What do Confucian and Buddhist teachings have to say about *haan*? While Korean folklore has recognized *haan* as a prevailing experience for a long time, *haan* or emotions like *haan*, are rarely mentioned in other Asian traditional literatures, including Oriental medicine. The Confucian traditions recognize various emotions; however, they emphasize the importance of having "proper four feelings," and using self-control so as not to arouse the "improper seven feelings." People were taught to control and suppress *haan* through self-discipline.

In Buddhism, we find a similar attitude. Buddhism tends to ignore *haan* and other human emotions, pointing out the impermanence and uselessness of emotion for the true self. This position can be easily understood, if one believes that all human suffering has its source in human desire, and that all emotions arise because of desires.

Contrary to these "high-minded" religions and teachings, we find a large number of references to *haan* in the popular folk traditions and shamanism. According to the Korean shamanism and folk beliefs, *haan* has been regarded as one of the prime causes of human suffering, illness and misfortunes. In fact, some claim that the Koreans' indigenous psychology is primarily the psychology of *haan* (SC Paik, 1993).

Shamans work with innocent or unfortunate *haan*ridden clients by offering care and healing. Korean shamanism uses complex forms of ritual called "*goot* (굿)." *Goot* ritual includes: invoking ancestral souls, dancing, chanting, narrating the patient' *haan*-ridden life story, and eventually going into a trance state. The *goot* is to resolve the dead's *haan* as well as that of the client. The process to release *haan* is called "*Haan-puri* (한풀이, unknot and let out *haan*)" (KT Lee. 1987). Almost all shamans are female and most of the clients are female. Commonly the female shaman herself has a history of a *haan*-ridden life herself, and becomes a shaman following her healing through help of another shaman. To be able to share one's deep feelings of *haan* with someone who has similar *haan* experiences is considered most helpful in the healing process.

There is one more side to *haan*. *Haan* can create and energize a strong motivation, not to give up, but to persevere and fight on until justice is done. It generates a driving force to do better, to excel, and to succeed in achieving goals, even if it takes a long time. It may also create a desire to get back at, and get even with, the oppressor and enemy who caused the *haan*.

Some Korean scholars have observed that the frequent anti-government demonstrations by college students in Seoul that include throwing fire-bottles are basically ritualistic expressions of their *haan* and *haan*-rage. Better educated and Western—acculturated Koreans, especially women and members of younger generations have become more verbally assertive and emotionally expressive without suppressing their feelings of anger and *haan*—related emotions.

O-GI 오기, 傲氣

O-gi is intense and concentrated desire and effort to conquer, surpass, and win over rivals in order to reach the goal of accomplishing success as a victory, such as in competition, fight, power struggle, or business objectives in retaliation against the individual(s) or circumstances which victimized and gave him or her the strong *haan* feelings and experiences. For example, the one who failed the business or college entrance examination in the past may double the efforts, based on *o-gi*, to succeed this time. The political party who lost the power struggle in the past may exert extra efforts to win next time. *O-gi* is based on the feelings of anger and *haan* related emotions.

Although Haan-based anger is dormant, long-term, indirect and underlying, "Ogi" is no longer underlying, and long term. It is compressed in time, energy and urgency. It is ready to energize the retaliatory, angry feeling for immediate deployment for revenge and 'sock it to it". Often Ogi comes after defeat, failure and loss, which represent a serious blow to one's ego, self-respect and self-esteem. Ogi provides extra—energy, stamina, motivation and determination, with the feelings that "no matter what, I will do it and a do it in achieving the goal." It is a rebound phenomenon of doubling of the energy.

Ogi is the sound of the way in which Koreans pronounce. But it actual come of the word "0-Ki." "O" means spiteful, malicious. "Ki" means "energy." Thus "Ogi" means spiteful, malicious negative energy. Ogi is a strong negative energy forceOgi is a universal psychological phenomenon which is often cited for reason for success following a failure in business.

Ogi is a driving force providing strong determination, spurt of super-power, energy and urgency to reach the goal. It can be extreme in extra effort and work in a sacrificial or super-human way. It can be a matter of making it or breaking it. In an extreme form, it can be a matter of life and death, no matter what.

If successful, the outcome can be spectacular and phenomenal. If failed, it can result in a tragedy equally in a spectacular manner.In the present Korea; there are strong desires and pressures for success spectacularly: in Chaebol, business, new products, sports (World Cup, Golf, base—ball, etc) and making a fortune.

CHE-MYUN 체면, 體面

Che-myun literally means "body and face," (낯, 면목, 위신) and refers to face-saving in the sense of saving social face or saving the external facade to maintain respectability. As in other Asian countries, face-saving behavior is very important to Koreans in their public and social relationship. Maintaining *che-myun* protects one's sense of dignity, self-respect, and respectability. Honor is an important concept to live by for Koreans, and the honor of the individual as well as his or her family is maintained through *che-myun*. *Che-myun* helps to promote harmonious relationships. For example, face-saving may help a person to behave more gracefully, and moderate his or her temper in facing a person, even if he or she is very angry at the person.

Che-myun also promotes the development of mutual obligations and responsibilities. If a person does not respond in a reciprocal manner, he or she loses face. If a person does you a favor, it is your turn to return the favor, Hence, *Che-myun* is conducive to the development of a reciprocal bond and mutual relationships between and among people. Asian societies historically have been very social status oriented. Therefore, generally Koreans/Asians are very conscious of their social status. That's why they like titles, honors, academic degrees from Ivy-league colleges, brand-name products, etc. People display *che-myun* behavior to maintain their social status, pride and prestige.

However, sometimes the *che-myun* behavior can be pretentious. If *che-myun* behavior is exaggerated, it can lead to a behavior of "*huh-seh* (허세, 虛勢)' or "*ki-mae* (き-まえ, 気前)" in Japanese. Huh-seh is similar to the Western concept of bravado or show-off. For example a person may assure oneself as well as others' status and prestige by driving a Mercedes and living in an expensive house in an exclusive area, even if he or she is actually living on a tight budget, In the spirit of *huh-seh*, one may give an expensive and extravagant party for friends, even if it means going into debt. Koreans especially are known for their very generous hospitality to house guests.

A concept related to *che-myun* is a behavior of *ab-dui* (앞뒤). In Korean *Ab* means "front," and *dui*, "back." It refers to presenting an external facade to a person's face, but behaves differently behind the other's back. This is similar to Takeo Doi's (1985) two fold theory of social consciousness of Japanese people. It is a behavior of "Otnote (おもて, 表) and Ura (うら, 裏): "external public display" and "internal private reality." This theme is often played symbolically in Asian theatrical dramas or dancing wearing carved wooden facial masks, such as in *Kabuki*, Korean *Tal-Choom*, and Chinese traditional opera. Carl Jung also spoke of a "persona," an external social person.

The behavior of *ab-dui* (front and back) represents a willful effort, perhaps sometimes desperately, to maintain a facade, not only to save one's own face, but to pay the courtesy of being pleasant or presenting one's best to the other person. An example is smiling to a person's face, while being angry with him or her inside oneself. It is difficult to be totally honest and open all the time, and to show one's real or raw feelings—especially when one wants to maintain social harmony and civility.

NOONCHI 눈치, (眼力见儿)

In Western culture, verbal communication is very important. It is emphasized that verbal communication be clear and explicit. However, in Asian culture, verbal communication is less clear, more subtle, indirect, and often non-verbal. Westerners who live in Korea often complain that Koreans are not communicative. A Korean may respond: "We, Koreans carry on conversations without talking. We can tell how you are thinking and feeling, without explaining it to us." Korea has been even called a "*noonchi* culture."

The Korean word *Noonchi* means literally "measuring with eyes." It is an intuitive, sixth-sense perception of another person—a capacity to size up and evaluate another person or situation quickly and intuitively. With *noonchi* one develops heightened awareness of, and sensitivity to another person's gestures, facial expressions, voice, the way of talking, body language, and other nonverbal cues.

In Asian countries, "honorific" language system is highly developed (SC Chang, 1988). Depending on whom you are talking to one uses different words and sentence structure. There are several words meaning "you," and which "you" one uses, defines the relationship between the addresser and addressee. It is somewhat similar to the German language which also has three different words for "you" and the speaker selects which word to use according to the level of intimacy or formality that is appropriate. There are also ways of "talking up" or "talking down" to the person.

Having an acute sense of *noonchi* is necessary and desirable in a hierarchical society where the emphasis is on observing the proper protocol and manners in interpersonal interactions. The intuitive ability of *noonchi* helps one discern where one stands in relation to a person or situation, since it is important to accord appropriate respect through the use of appropriate language and manner. In order to live in peace and harmony with people in crowded housing in a congested city, one needs to scrutinize others and accommodate their needs and feelings as much as possible. Hence, to describe a person as being without *noonchi* is a derogatory remark. It implies that the person is insensitive, uncouth, unmannered, and uncultured. In other words, he is a jerk.

On the other hand, excessive *noonchi* may be a sign of insecurity, hypersensitivity, and possible anxiety. If carried to an extreme, clinical manifestations of social phobia and paranoia may occur. A culture-related subtype of social phobia, called "*Taein-Kongpo* (TK, 대인공포, 對人恐怖)" in Korean, and "*Taijin-kyofu*" in Japanese, has been of great interest among Asian psychiatrists. Examples of TK symptoms include: fear of blushing, fear of one's hands shaking when writing in front of someone, fear of bad breath or body odor offending someone, fear of gazing (i.e. fear that one's gaze might be seen as too sharp, fierce and threatening to others,) fear of being embarrassed and humiliated with a physical defect, etc. TK is considered to be related to excessive cultural emphasis on *noonchi* (SH Lee 1993b, 1995c).

PALJA 팔자, 八字

Palja means "fate" or "destiny," and is derived from terminology used in fortune telling. In the traditional Korean and Asian societies, a person's role and life status were essentially predetermined, not only by one's gender and birth order, but also by one's social status, role, and the position accorded by one's family status and heritage. Individuals had little control over their lives. Using the modern psychological terminology, one's locus of control is not within oneself, but in the hands of fate and destiny.

How were people to cope with their misfortunes not of their own making? They were to accept their fate with a stoic, fatalistic, or religious and philosophical attitude: "That is my *palja*," "That is my fate." In the old days, acceptance of one's own *palja* was probably the only option available.

244   LUKE KIM, M.D., PH.D.

Going along with fate through non-action, and accepting the nature the way it is, is the essence of Taoism (SC Chang, 1982). This is one of the strong reasons why religions, such as Buddhism, Taoism, Shamanism, and the philosophy of Confucianism have appealed to and thrived among so many Koreans.

Religions help people cope with woes of life and accept their *palja* more readily. But now better educated. younger generations do not adopt stoicism and fatalism as did older generations. Nonetheless, because historically Koreans have suffered a lot, the idea of *palja* has a firm hold among Koreans.

With the beginning of the 20th century, people all over the world developed such a strong confidence and faith in the advancement of science and technology that people thought that human kind can chart the course of nature and can solve all the problems at hand with science and technology. I think the arrogance of science has emerged. In recent years, however, people have begun to realize the limitation as well as potential destructiveness of science and technology. People begin to have more awareness of ecological issues and respect for nature. Earthquakes, natural calamities, the unchanging viciousness of human nature, unsolved medical diseases, such as cancer, immune disorders, genetic factors in many diseases, etc., all point to the power of Nature, in spite of the scientific efforts to harness and control Nature. Even in the U.S., people are now beginning to talk more about fate, acceptance and surrender. The rapid increase of conservative Christian movement and the popular books, such as "Care of the Soul" (T Moore, 1992) reflect the new mood and awareness of the limitation of a human's own power and self-sufficiency. *Palja* is still alive and well.

MUHT 멋, (表现美)

Muht is a Korean word used to describe the quality of being "exquisite, beautiful, splendid, refined, or elegant." A person of *muht* is someone who knows how to enjoy life; someone who appreciates nature, art, music, and poetry. That person is likely to enjoy good food, wine, refined clothes, and may be even good-looking. Hence, people like to date or marry such a person of *muht* taste.

The ethos of *muht* probably promotes the development of exquisite musical, artistic and other cultural tastes and appreciation among Koreans.

Koreans love music—especially singing—even when they are sad. Koreans are regarded as very artistic and musical, and Korea has produced some world-class musicians. For the many Koreans who have had a painful history of war, suffering, and *haan*. the goal of having a *muht*—rich life is a hope and desire for them to attain.

REFERENCE

1. Ahn SM: Personal communication (doctoral dissertation on *haan*, Emory University,1992).
2. APA DSM IV Committee: Diagnostic And Statistical Manual IV. Washington DC, American Psychiatric Press, 1994.
3. Baker-Miller J: Toward A New Psychology of Women. Boston, Beacon, 1976.
4. Cha JH: Aspects of individualism and collectivism in Korea. In Individualism and Collectivism: Theory,Method. AndApplications. Edited by Kim UC, Triandis HC, Kagitcibasi C, Choi SC, Yoon G. Thousand Oaks, London New Delhi,1994.
5. Chang SC: The nature of the self: a transcultural view, Part 1: theoretical aspects. Transcultural Psychiatric Research Review 25(3): 169-203, 1988.
6. Choi KS: The *Haan* of Korean People. Seoul, Korea, Jeyunsa Publisher, 1991(in Korean).
7. Choi SC, Kim U, Choi SH : Indigenous analysis of collective representation: a Korean perspective. In indigenous Psychologies: Research and Experience in cultural Context. Edited by Kim U, Berry JW. Newbury Park London New Dehli, Sage Publ. 1993.
8. Choi SJ: Korean psychology of Shim-*jeong*: a study of the experiential aspect of *jeong* and *haan*. Paper presented at the Korean Psychological Association Sympoium on Korean Characteristics: psychological explorations, Seoul National University,Seoul, Korea, October 22, 1993 (in Korean).
9. Doi T: The Anatomy of Dependence. Tokyo & New York, Kodansha International, 1981.
10. Doi T: The Anatomy of Self: the Individual Versus Society. Tokyo & New York, Kodansha International, 1985.
11. Galligan C: In A Different Voice. Cambridge, MA, Harvard University Press, 1982.

12. Kim L: Psychiatric care of Korean Americans, in Culture. Ethnicity and Mental Illness. Edited by Gaw A. Washington, DC, American Psychiatric Press, 1992, pp347-412.

13. Kim L: Korean ethos: concept of *Jeong* and *Haan*. Paper presented at Winter meeting of American Academy o Psychoanalysis, San Antonio. TX, 1990.

14. Kim U: Individualism and collectivism: conceptual clarification and elaboration. In Individualism And Collectivism: Theory, Method, And Application. Edited by Kim U, Triandis HC. Ka.c.,iycibasi C. Choi SC. & Yoon, G. Thousand Oaks, London and New Delhi, Sage Publications, 1994, p19-40.

15. Kohut H: The Restoration of Self. New York, International Universities Press, 1977.

16. Lebra TS: Japanese Patterns of Behavior. Honolulu, Hawaii, University of Hawaii Press, 1976.

17. Lee KT: Han purl moo (The dance for Unknotting Han), Chosun Daily News, July 11.1987.

18. Lee KW: Personal communication, 1995.

19. Lee SH: A study of the "Hwabyung—(Anger syndrome). J of Korea General Hospital 1 (2): 63-69.

20. Lee SH: Taein-Kongpo. Seoul, Korea, Ilchoszak Publisher, 1993 (in Korean).

21. Lee SH: Social phobia and Taein-Kongpo. Paper presented at the annual meeting of Korean Neuropsychiatric Association, Seoul, Korea, 1995.

22. Lee SW, Lee HN: Socio-psychological study of Korean in-*jeong*. Paper presented at the Korean PsychologicalAssociation Symposium on Korean Characteristics: psychological explorations. Oct.22, 1993, Seoul National University, Seoul, Korea.

23. LeVine RA: Infant environment in psychoanalysis: a cross-cultural view. In Cultural Psychology: Essays on Comparative Human Development, Edited by JW Singler, RA Shweder, and G Herdi. New York. Cambridge University Press, 1990.

24. Lin KM: *Hwa-byung*: a Korean culture-bound syndrome? Am J Psychiatry, 140(1):105-107, 1983.

25. Min SK, Lee HY: A diagnostic study on Hwabyung, I of the Korean Medical Association, 29: 653-661, 1986.

26. Paik SC: The Hahn and Korean Disease Pang KY: Hwabyung: the construction of a Korean popular illness among Korean elderly

immigrant women in the United States. Culture, Medicine and Psychiatry 14:495-512.

27. Park ES: Personal communication, 1995

28. Prince RH: Review on a diagnostic study of Hwabyung by Min SK, Lee HY. Transcultural Psychiatric Research Review, 26: 137-147, 1989.

29. Prozan CK: Feminist Psychoanalytic Psychotherapy. Northvale, NJ, Jason Aronson, 1992.

30. Sinha D, Tripathi RC: Individualism in a collectivistic culture: a case of coexistence of opposites. In Individualism and Collectivism: Theory, Method. And Applications. Edited by Kim U, Triandis HC, Kagiycibasi C, Choi SC, & Yoon, G. Thousand Oaks, London and New Delhi, Sage Publications, 1994, p123-136.

31. Winnicott DW: The Maturational Processes And The Facilitating Environment. New York, International Universities, 1965.

32. Winnicott DW: Holding And Interpretation: Fragment of An Analysis. New York, Grove Press, 1986.

33. Yu KH, Kim L: The growth and development of Korean American children, in Psychosocial Development of Minority Children. Edited by Johnson-Powell G, Yamamoto J, Romero A. New York, Brunnel/Mazel, 1983, pp 147-158.

7. East and West difference

Asian Traditional Values	Western Values
Expressive modes	**Expressive modes**
- self-effacing	- self-promoting
- non-verbal, indirect, implicit	- verbal, explicit
- no eye contact	- eye contact
- no body contact, bow	- physical contact, hugging
- sex private	- kissing in public
- non-expression of feelings	- free and overt expression of feelings
- deferential, polite, humble	- self-assured, self-assertive
- goal-directed	- spontaneous

Family

- We-oriented
- duty and obedience
- family royalty, solidarity
- peace and harmony of the family
- filial piety, vertical relationship
- submission, accommodation, acceptance
- ascribed status and role i.e. husband/wife
- parent-son bond stressed
- family discipline for deviation via shame/guilt/punishment
- unconditional love during early child rearing (Amaeru)

Family

- I-oriented
- freedom of choice and self-determinism
- individual pursuit of happiness
- individual happiness
- horizontal relationship
- confrontation and challenge if necessary
- democratic/achieved status
- husband-wife bond stressed
- reliance on public agencies for discipline
- emphasis on the training of independence in child-earing

Values

- success thru self-discipline and will power
- sense of fatalism, stoicism or resignation in the face of adversity
- and obligation
- collective problem-solving, consensus-building
- inter-dependency
- achievement-oriented, status conscious
- holistic: living in harmony with nature

Values

- pragmatism and exploitation of opportunity
- sense of optimism
- avoidance of obligation
- individual problem-solving
- autonomy, independence
- self-actualization
- man's need to control nature
- mental health thru expression of feelings
- mental illness as a result of psychological conflicts and biological factors
- free expression o[psychological conflicts
- belief that psychotherapy promotes self-growth
- long-term intensive psychotherapy favored

FMental Health and Illness

- mental health thru will power and avoidance of morbid thought
- mental illness as imbalance of cosmic forces, Yin-Yang, or supernatural event, i.e. demon possession
- emphasis on reciprocity physical symptoms and somatic complaints as manifestations of emotional problems
- medication is preferred to talk-therapy
- directive, active therapy Kith limited goal is preferred
- Asian-Pacific patients need less dosage of psychotropic medication than Caucasians

Mental Health and Illness

- mental health thru expression of feelings
- mental illness as a result of psychological conflicts and biological factors
- free expression o[psychological conflicts
- belief that psychotherapy promotes self-growth
- long-term intensive psychotherapy favored

8. Therapeutic approach of Jeong-based relationships

Luke Kim, MD, Ph.D.
University of California Davis School of Medicine

A therapeutic application of Jeong is not a particular techniques or method. But, rather it is an attitude, frame of reference, mindset and value orientation in dealing with people in our human relationships. Jeong is a concept prevalent in the Korean/Asian traditional culture.

I work at a county-contracted community mental health clinic located in Galt about 15 miles south of Sacramento. It is a small rural town surrounded by open land. The clinic has about 10 full time interdisciplinary mental health professional staff including a clinic manager and 2 front desk office workers. I am the only psychiatrist. The clinic has about 300 cases to take care of as case load: 240 adults and 60 children. About 50 % are chronic schizophrenia and bipolar disorders, with the rest consisting of major depression, anxiety and phobic disorders. The majority are Caucasian patients.

With the cooperation of the staff, I have attempted to create a Jeong—based office practice and staff interpersonal relationships, at least based on a conceptual and conscious level.

I shared and discussed with the staff on the concept of Jeong. They seemed curious, informed, interested, appreciative, and enlightened.

Jeong-based office practice with the staff is characterized by: 1) emphasis on warm, kind and positive interpersonal relationship among staff, 2) mutual interest in personal growth and career opportunities, like you would have for your brothers and sisters. 3) the feeling of "We"—togetherness as a team, 4) family-like bonding,

In my assessment, office work has become much more pleasant and smooth. The staff morale has been high. They feel happier and satisfied in their social and emotional interactions. The staff turnover rate is low except for promotional or better opportunities.

One might ask how Jeong-based office practice is different from any other well managed office. Probably not. It is the conscious effort and attitude, sharing of the common framework and goal, desire for a family-like team work and mutual bonding. It is much less bureaucratic, impersonal, business-like, and individually oriented, and competitive efficiency model. It is rather a warm, "we together," family-like human relations model. Talking about the concept of Jeong was helpful toward unifying the effort of team work.

One might ask that it may work because it is a small clinic. Probably it will equally work well if the organizational operation is divided into subunits of manageable size in a larger system, applying a system theory approach.

In my clinical work, I have many chronically impaired schizophrenic patients who show flat and expressionless affect, apathy, social withdrawal, restricted interest and life style. I feel that they need to be treated with respect, human dignity, empowerment, and affection like a family member, in addition to a good effective treatment with medication.

To promote an optimal therapeutic engagement, I have tried to apply the concept of Jeong-based therapeutic relations by: (1) showing active interest, caring attitude, and attention to the individual in a way that it may create affectively more comfortable and caring emotional relationship. 2) To make them feel more secure with the continuity and stability of our relationship, and 3) too instill the feelings of hope with "we can work together."

Of course, I do not use this approach with all patients, being aware of certain paranoid patients who may feel uncomfortable and afraid of being too close to people.

In my experience, the great majority of the patients appear to appreciate and welcome such opportunity and experience because most of them have a personal history of neglected, deprived, deficient or almost non-existence of personally meaningful emotional relationships with anyone in their life.

How is the Jeong-based approach different from empathy? Perhaps similar except to say that: 1) my empathic listening to not only here and now, but also interested in developing a long term relationship and bonding, 2) Interest in making them feel more secure of the continuity and stability in our relationship. 3) I am more conscious of developing "we" feeling and relationship—"let's do solve this together, let's work on this thing together."

I try to avoid a business-like, stand-offish, neutral or routine, perfunctory professional manner, which may not have enough time beyond the busy schedule of medication prescription writing.

Also I am trying to avoid the often directly or indirectly communicated message in the mental health counseling that "it's your problem; you have to figure it out, you have to deal with it yourself, and you need to come up with our own answer."

You might ask, aren't you encouraging the development of dependency on you? Perhaps some initially, as I would teach my growing children by doing things together initially and gradually encourage him/her to do alone later.

9. Association of Korean American Psychiatrists (AKAP) Activities

[9 A] Paper presented on October 8, 1994 at AKAP California Society in LA

PSYCHOTHERAPY AND SPIRITUALITY
(Paper presented on 10-8-94 at AKAP California Society in LA)

Luke I. C. Kim, MD

BIO-PSYCHO-SOCIAL MODEL OF PSYCHIATRY:

The APA officially adopted the bio-psycho-social model of psychiatry about fifteen years ago. However, psychiatry is still divided into two camps, biological psychiatry and psychodynamic psychiatry, with each side accusing the opponent of emphasizing the **mindless brain** on one hand, and the **brainless mind** on the other. However, until recently psychiatry has avoided or ignored another important area, **spirituality, faith and beliefs.**

Up until fifteen to twenty years ago, the APA frowned on any proposal for symposiums on religion or spirituality in the annual scientific meetings. However, things have changed. In the 1992 APA Annual Meeting, a special lecture was given by Dr. Scott Peck, MD, author of the book, "The Road Less Traveled," on the topic of spirituality, and the huge auditorium was jam-packed with standing room only. There is a ground swell of demand for therapy or counseling on spiritual issues across the American population in the last few years. There are many popular books published these days on spirituality. For example, Thomas Moor's books "Care of the Soul" and "Soul Mate" have been best sellers for many months.

Why is there new interest in spirituality? Is it a reflection of what's happening in the society and in the lives of millions of average citizens? The "good old days" of American fun-loving, easygoing, painless and affluent society are gone. During last several years, the United States has witnessed drastic decline in the overall quality of life, including significant economic hardships, unemployment, family breakdown, deterioration of social and personal values, and increasing crime and violence, etc. When people are in pain and suffering without much relief, they tend to become more serious and spiritual, as we become more spiritual when we are facing death, such as terminal cancer.

Also severe budget cuts in public social and mental health services, as well as managed care services in psychiatry has forced mental health professions to look for or innovate treatment strategies that are more cost effective and more helpful to patients. While newer psychotropic medications have improved in the treatment of mentally ill, consumers are still afraid of side-effects of medication. Psychotherapy can be helpful but labor-intensive and expensive.

For whatever reason, many people seem to have become interested more in spirituality. Especially the younger and educated generations are fascinated by Eastern thoughts, Eastern religions, meditation and ways of dealing with pain and suffering.

I learned that during and soon after the Vietnam War, there were only five trained Vietnamese psychiatrists in a population of thirty million. They did not have psychologists and psychiatric social workers either. I asked a Vietnamese psychiatrist how the Vietnamese people were able to cope with the tremendous stress and distress of going through the protracted war, destruction, war injury, loss of families members, and their suffering and pain. He replied: "They coped with and survived, not by therapy or medication, but by the strength of religious beliefs, a certain life attitude and philosophy."

In Western psychiatry, we have medicalized human suffering and misery, and tried to treat medically and psychotherapeutically the human misery, and thus society has created a massive production of mental health professionals.

[9 B] Newsletter article on Psychiatry and Spirituality on March 14, 2000

(Article contributed to the "Visionary" Newsletter, Visions Unlimited, Sacramento CA) 3/14/2000

Psychiatry and Spirituality

Luke Kim MD, staff psychiatrist

During the last two or three decades, there has been a tremendous advancement of neuroscience, a study of the brain, its functions and brain chemistry. As a result we have many more effective and newer psychiatric medications, for example, Risperdal or Prozac. Human happiness, depression, human conflicts, predicaments and misery are becoming more medicalized. Biological psychiatry trends to reduce all human behaviors to the final pathway of brain chemistry and neurotransmitters, such as Dopamine and Serotonin. Thus the solution is to fix "the brain chemistry imbalance" with a proper adjustment of the neurotransmitters or with a blocking agent of the neurotransmitters in the hopes that it will lead to an ever happy and heavenly life in the process, it ignores other dimensions of humanity: the mind, heart, culture and spirituality.

The Gallop poll revealed that ninety percent of the US population said they believe in God. Nevertheless, psychiatry failed to pay attention to the spiritual needs of people. In fact, traditional psychiatry had a negative attitude toward religion. When psychiatric patients mention religious themes, mental health professionals tend to view them as religious delusions or symptoms of mental illness. Certainly some psychiatric symptoms may be manifested as religious delusion or hallucinations, but a desire for religious journey and spiritual quest is to be honored as part of the human needs.

What is spirituality? Spiritually may or may not overlap with religion. We may be concerned with something large than ourselves, or seek connection with something beyond ourselves (transpersonal), whether it is the Source, god or universe. I feel spiritual when I experience a sense of awe and wonder with the beauty, vastness and mystery of the nature and universe. I feel spiritual when I listen to the great music of Bach and Beethoven. I think they are the work of their spiritual creation. I see the splendor of nature in a wild flower at the edge of the street fence. It is an existential and spiritual question when we are asking the meaning and purpose of our life. When we face a crisis, our family member dies or we have a terminal illness, we are more likely to ask existential and spiritual questions.

In psychiatry, medication management and psychotherapy are the main treatment approaches. Medications help to diminish or get rid of psychiatric symptoms. Psychotherapy help to resolve the childhood trauma, emotional or sexual abuse, and to clarify, understand and resolve the past and present conflicts. Psychotherapy helps to improve coping, social, and communication skills.

10. The CAPITAL and CAPITAL Foundation's Luke and Grace Kim "Profiles of Courage" Award

This award is a very special award. It is not an annual award. It is not an award to be given out lightly. This award is to be representative of the people it was named after—Luke and Grace Kim. It is an award that is to epitomize and capture the very essence of Luke and Grace Kim—courage, heart, sacrifice, love of community and selflessness.

This award is to epitomize courage. When the Russian occupied North Korea, they imposed communism on the North Korean. Luke Kim and his classmates decided to protest and demonstrate against the oppression of the Russian Communists. Russian planes strafed and machine gunned the demonstrators killing 20 to 25 and wounding numerous students. This massacre occurred in 1946 and Luke Kim was 15 years old.

This award is to epitomize heart and sacrifice. When you see the twinkling eyes and shy smile of Dr. Luke Kim and the kind and gentle face of Grace Kim, you would never know the horrors, pain and sufferings they endured in their lifetime. Both Luke and Grace's family fled North Korea into South Korea to escape the Communist oppression. When the North Korean Army invaded South Korea they hunted down those who escaped from North Korea. Luke's mother was arrested, taken away and never seen again by her children. Grace hid in the countryside for over 2 months to evade the North Koreans. Luke lived underground in a coffin like space under a closet in a house to escape detection by the North Koreans. During this period of their lives, they survived numerous harrowing experiences which could be described as miraculous. They were separated for over six years before they were able to reunite and married.

This award is to epitomize love of community. Luke and Grace Kim have spent their entire lives in making a difference in their community—not just the Korean community but for all communities. It is Grace Kim receiving hate mails and death threats because she dared to advocate for the ordination of eligible gays and lesbians to church office. Both Luke and Grace believe the gay I lesbian issue is one of civil rights and not a moral question of right or wrong.

This award is to epitomize selflessness. It is the giving without measure of their time, knowledge, wisdom and money to the community to the extent that Luke and Grace Kim mortgaged their home to pay for the legal defense of a young man they believed to be wrongfully convicted of murder and incarcerated in prison for life. This young man today, Chol Sol Lee has a second chance at life today because of Luke and Grace Kim.

It is for all of those reason that makes this award very special because it is named for Luke and Grace Kim, who are very special people in our community,—who have made a difference in all of our lives—and who have made this world a better place for all of us to live in. All of us are so happy and thrilled that Luke and Grace have returned from their retirement home in Los Angeles to make this first and very special presentation tonight to our honoree.

Now to tell you tonight about the honoree and recipient of the Luke and Grace Kim "Profile of Courage" Award, we have Alice Wong, the President of the CAPITAL Foundation and Captain Brian Louie from the Sacramento Police Dept.

Given June 24, 2006 by Jerry L. Chong,
CAPITAL & CAPITAL Foundation
Black Tie Gala "in Every Heart"
Radisson Hotel, Sacramento, California

11. Presbyterian Church Award for Grace Kim

Women of Faith Breakfast

Honoring Deacons, Elders and Clergywomen

Sunday, June 18, 2006
8:00-10:00 A.M.
The Sheraton Hotel
Birmingham, Alabama

Sponsored by the Women's Ministries Area
National Ministries Division
217th General Assembly (2006)
Presbyterian Church (USA)

Grace S. Kim

A third generation Presbyterian, I was born and raised in Shanghai, China. My Korean parents moved to China in the 1920s as a result of Japan's colonization of Korea. In 1945, my family returned to North Korea. There we discovered an intolerable communist regime with no freedom of worship. The family escaped to South Korea. We settled in Seoul where I enrolled in Seoul National University. The Korean War broke out in 1950; the North Korean Arm invaded South Korea.

We narrowly escaped. I hid in the countryside for two months until UN Forces retook Seoul. We returned to Seoul, and I volunteered at an orphanage to care for the young people there. I reenrolled at Seoul National University and received a bachelor of art degree in education. I immigrated to the United States in 1962 and married Luke, a psychiatrist, in Buffalo, New York. After moving to California, I received a master's degree in human development and educational counseling at Cal Poly State University in San Luis Obispo, California.

I taught school for 24 years at Davis Senior High School in Davis, California, and retired in 1996. I developed a curriculum in family life, focusing on interpersonal relations and personal growth (life skills, human sexuality, substance abuse, and so on). Before and during retirement, I became actively involved in church activities and community service.

Until moving to Los Angeles three months ago, I was an elder at Davis Community Church PC (USA). I served on the PC(USA) General Assembly Nominating Committee, and I was active with Asian Presbyterian Women and the Ethnic Concerns Committee of Sierra Mission Partnership in the Synod of the Pacific.

Throughout the years, I have held leadership positions in a variety of organizations and causes; vice-chair of the National Defense Committee to Save Chol Soo Lee; president of the Sacramento Korean American Community Association; and board member/adviser for organizations such as CAPITAL (a coalition of organizations in Northern California), Korean Adoptee & Adoptive Family Network, and the Korean American Coalition.

I have worked as a weekly columnist for ethnic Korean newspapers and as co-editor of Currents (a newspaper serving the Asian Pacific Islander community.) Luke and I have two sons and four grandchildren. My faith journey has been inspired and strengthened by Jesus' command: love your neighbor as yourself, including those who are poor, sick, voiceless, marginalized and oppressed.

12. Article on Ethnic Concerns Committee

Remember! Renew! Rejoice!

A Celebration of 30 Years of Racial Ethnic Advocacy in Sierra Mission Area, Church & Society, Presbyterian Church (USA) Vol. 93 No. 3 pp 62-70, 2003

Luke & Grace Kim

Historically, agricultural work in California's Central Valley has been carried out by Hispanic and Asian Pacific farmers and laborers, such as Filipinos and Japanese. Chinese laborers excavated the rugged Sierra Montains for railroads and tunnels. In more recent years, a large influx of the Southeast Asian population, especially Hmong and Cambodian have settled in the area.

California is increasingly multi-cultural and multi-lingual, with Sacramento now considered the most racially diverse city in the nation.

According to the 2000 Census, Sacramento's half million population consists of: White 48.3%, Hispanic 21.5%, Asian American 16.6%, African American 15.5%, Nataive American 1.3%, Native Hawaiian and Pacific Islanders 0.9% and two or more mised races of color 6.4%

Spiritual and social service needs are urgent for new immigrants in the area, who experience marginalization, adjustment difficulty and emotional struggles, along with feelings of alienation, underemployment, language barriers and cultural conflicts. To these people, Christian faith and ethnic churches offer a sense of hope, spiritual strength and fellowship.

In the Sierra Mission Area of California, the Ethnic Concerns Committee (ECC) became the vehicle to address these people's needs and spiritual hunger

ECC: The Beginnings

In 1972, following the reorganization of the denominational structure by General Assembly, the newly reconstituted regional synods were mandated to form ethnic ministry councils or organizations within their structures. Overture 141 from Philadelphia Presbytery, which created this mandate read in part:

> Each new regional synod shall provide an instrumentally for its ministry among the ethnic minorities . . . within its bounds (Asian Americans, Hispanic Americans, Indian Americans and Black Americans) . . . In order to guarantee that such a ministry be strengthened, an instrumentality to be adminstered by ethnic minority personnel and with budgeted financial resources (shall) be instituted with the following responsibilities:
>
> (a) To initiate and implement plans, strategies, and program which are designed to meet the needs, consistent with the gospel, of ethnic ministries; (and)
> (b) To allocate the budgeted funds for carrying out this ministry.

Since then, each regional area has been encouraged to respond and formulate an organization (ethnic caucus, task force, committee, etc.) based on their own needs and composition.

In response to the mandate, the Sierra Mission Area Administrative Council approved the organizing of an Ethnic Consultation, which was held in Galt, CA in September 1973. Out of that initial consultation emerged the Ethnic Concerns Committee (ECC), which represented nine ethnic backgrounds and churches: Japanese, Chinese, Korean, Filipino, Black, Native American, Latino/Hispanic, Assyrian, and Armenian. ECC caucuses have since increased with the addition of Indonesian and Vietnamese members, as well as the participation of youth and young adults from Southeast Asia through the Fresno Interdenominational Refugee Ministry (FIRM).

The purpose of the consultation was to share ethnic concerns and to explore ways of Christian outreach meaningful to ethnic persons in the Sierra Mission Area. The ECC became an arm of the Sierra Mission Area office and worked closely with Robert Graham, Executive Presbyter, and Bryce Little, Ministries Consultant for the Mission Area.

Bryce Little, having been a missionary to Thailand and Singapore for nine years, knew how to work with Asian Pacific Christians, and it is generally agreed that his presence was instrumental in helping to chart and shape the direction of ECC activities and projects. As a committed, inspiring and creative enabler, he generated much of the spirit and enthusiasm, gently guiding and pushing, and establishing coordination and networking among marginalized and inexperienced racial ethnic Presbyterians, many of whom were recent immigrants.

ECC Development

ECC has touched many lives and provided ECC members with opportunities for an active and sustained faith journey, personal growth and leadership development. With nurturing and suportive encouragement, marginalized ethnic minority Christians have grown, developed and emerged as more confident and dedicated church servants and prominent leaders in the PCUSA.

Early on, ECC developed a framework of goals as follows:

- Develop an understanding of who we are as ethnic Christians for our own personal growth and spiritual development.

- Study the ethnic and cultural heritage of specific groups and strengthen the commonality of the Christian experiences.

- Assist in widening the understanding of our Christian faith in a multi-ethnic and multi-cultural society, which is brought together through mutual respect and love in Jesus Christ; and share the varieties and uniqueness of the ethnic perspective that speaks to the whole church.

- Assist, support and strengthen the work of the special needs of the Presbyterian ethnic groups: new ethnic church development, ethnic ministries, eethnic caucuses, consulting committees, consultation and counseling, as well as youth ministry.

- Develop leadership for ethnic youth and adult Presbyterians in the denomination.

- Develop a talent and resource bank of ethnic persons to serve on the General Assembly, synod, presbytery, committees and other entities.

- Participate in the decision making processes in every judicatory level.

- Develop ethnic-related church school curriculum, teaching material and library resources to share for the enrichment of the Church.

- Develop and publish ethnic oral histories: i.e. Japanese, Korean and Filipino, and share their life stories and faith journey.

- Compile information and data on ethnic ministries in North America.

The 30ᵗʰ Anniversary Gathering

This past October, ECC celebrated thirty years of racial ethnic ministry development at Zephyr Point, Lake Tahoe, Nevada under the leadership of ECC chair Maria Yee. Gathered by the theme "Remember! Renew! Rejoice!" about 150 people came together. Young and old, current and former ECC members participated: celebrating and sharing their faith journey as well as personal stories of how their ECC experiences shaped, changed and transformed their lives and spiritual passage.

In the beautiful environment of the spectacular Lake Tahoe and Sierra Mountains, with wonderful instrumental music, singing and cultural performances, this joyful reunion was indeed an exuberant, mountaintop experience for all who participated.

In remembering and reviewing what EEC has done during the last 30 years, the consultation rejoiced in ECC's many remrkable accomplishments.

1. Korean new church development, already strong in Sacramento, was strengthened in Renovation, Las Vegas, Stockton, Fresno, Modesto, and Bakersfield. A multi-cultural approach to African American new church development was initiated in South Sacramento.

2. ECC encouraged Native American churchs to come together, resulting in a synod-wide Native American coalition that is still functioning today. We were a galvanizing force. Also Hispanic fellowships have developed in Stockton and San Joaquin Presbyteries.

3. Under the leadership of Rev Hei Takarabe, ECC took the initiative and funded oral history projects. The project quickly evolved into a Japanese oral history project, a Filipino oral history project, and a Korean oral history project. These oral projects wonderful, historical publications (five or six books). They are still continuing, especially the Korea oral history in preparation for the upcoming centennial celebration of Korean immigration in 2003. The projects helped racial ethnic young people get excited by discovering their cultural roots and heritage and learning about their early

immigrants, their hardship, struggle, survival and courage. Starting from her college days, for example, Joan Cordova did the oral history of Filipino early immigrants, and published a book, Voice.

4. ECC initiated a program of crisis counseling for Asian-born wives of US military servicemen. Alice Nishi and Grace Kim proposed and were granted funds for this much-needed ministry of counseling for Asian-born spouses near the military and airbases who were having serious marital and family crises due to language and cultural factors. The counselors responded to crises night and day for five years. They published an annotated bibliography on interracial marriage. At the end of the funding period, the project was turned over to a Sacramento county funded agency.

5. The Chol Soo Lee case was a very exciting and inspiring five year chapter in our work from 1978 to 1983. It is a complicated story but to make it short, Lee was a Korean immigrant youth who could not speak English and who had been arrested and imprisoned on a murder charge. A nationally known Korean American newspaper reporter, Mr. K.W. Lee, who was convinced of Chol Soo's innocence after a six month independent investigation, approached active ECC Korean members, particularly Jay Yoo (a UC Davis law student and how an assemblyman in the Republic of Korea) and Grace Kim, a high school teacher, who were convinced that it was an important social justice issue to stand for. Both of them became the leaders of the national defense committee for Chol Soo Lee, which was made possible through seed money from the Presbyterian Social Justice Funds.

Wide publicity of the case hit the raw nerves of many immigrant youth, as well as Korean and other ethnic Christians, who suddenly understood that any Asian was vulnerable to arrest based on "all look alike mistaken identity" as was the case with Chol Soo Lee. Members in ECC spearheaded a nationwide campaign for his defense, which truly became a pan-Asian movement in this country. The campaign spread across college campuses on both coasts, and support for the defense fund came from all over the country.

After a five-year legal battle in which he was ultimately found to be innocent, ECC succeeded in obtaining Chol Soo Lee's freedom. Inspired by this experience of social justice advaocay, at least ten Asian American college students decided to go to law school.

As Bryce Little reflects on the effort:

> . . . ECC came together to help the movement to save his life. Through the hearings they attended day after day, recent Asian immigrants learned a lot about the American legal system, especially the jury system.

6. Year after year there have been wonderful ministries and outreach to youth, offering ethnic youth summer camps, scholarships to Youth Triennium, etc. Youth ministry leader Joyce Uyeda is full of energy. Rev. Mary Paik, who is now Vice President of Student Affairs at McCormick Theological Seminary, is an example of the youth who came through these programs.

"Being created in the image of God means that every peron is an heir to a legacy of dignity and worth. Image of God calls us to resist self-negation. Being created in God's image heals us in the midst of suffering and enables us to experience love in the midst of hate. In the image of God, hopes shows up in the midst of despair, and life is born in the midst of death, thereby empowering us to struggle, to exist, to grow and prevail in the midst of chaos and destructive force."

Rev. Helen Locklear, Associate Director, Racial Ethnic Program Area, National Ministries Division, PCUSA and keynote speaker at the 30th anniversary ECC consultation.

---

7. New immigrants keep coming, and in keeping with the advice of Romans 12:13 ("contribute to the needs of the saints, extend hospitality to strangers") ECC continues to reach out to strangers and new groups who are often invisible to our communities. The 2000 census demographics guide us as we reach out and encourage new residents to become part of our family in ECC.

Sharing Stories from the ECC Journey

The story of ECC is best told in the words of the persons whose lives were so deeply intertwined with that of the effort. Here are a few:

"Historically in the treaty agreement, American Indians had only one choice. That is to become a Christian. Decision as to . . . denomination .. was decided for us by the US government. Government and church organizations decided on where ministry would occur. We were not the author of the decision.

"Because American Indians always had a spiritual life and had a belief about the creator, which parallels somewhat to the Bible, it is not difficult for American Indians to accept Christianity, even though it was imposed upon them. Many American Indians saw the value of being a Christian, and willingly joined a denomination, whether it was Presbyterian, Eposcopal or Catholic, or whatever!

"Prior to the 141 Overture, the doors had been pretty much closed for racial ethnic people in decision making process. Credentials were not looked at equally. 141 opened the door to some extent and provided an opportunity to many of us to move forward, including an opportunity to be employed at the national level . . .

Elder Ralph Scissons: ECC charter member,
and a national leader of the American Indian
Presbyterian Caucus and community

"Our challenge and commitment is to enliven community and enliven richness in the great tapestry of our Presbyterian traditions and faith community, regardless of who you are and where you come from."

Alice Nishi: ECC charger member, and a
national leader of Presbyterian Women and
numerous other national committees.

"I was insecure, poor in English and afraid to speak up in public. However, through involvement in ECC activities and committee work, I have learned a lot. I acquired the experience of conducting meetings with the Roberts rules. I benefited from the opportunities to express and exchange my ideas and issues in a small committee setting. I developed and enjoyed friendship and fellowship. These experiences helped me develop my confidence, improve my interpersonal and communication skills and leadership.

"One opportunity led to another with a snowballing effect for me, giving me different leadership experiences. ECC trained me and transformed my life, and deepened my Christian faith . . .

Grace Kim: ECC charter member and a member of GA Nominating Committee.

"We may feel powerful here, and we have the opportunity to serve the church and serve other people. But sometimes we cannot really answer the call unless there are some people in the position and power in the decision making who can help facilitate the process also. We have been very fortunate in the Sierra Mission area. We had staff people that strongly supported Overture 141 when it was passed. They took the 141 issue seriously and did not let it die."

"Bob Graham, then the executive Presbyter, saw the light and hope and had his staff make sure that they put some energy and money into this 141 mandate. Also we are very fortunate to have Bryce Little, a dynamite kind of person, with a lot of energy and enthusiasm. Without them, we wouldn't be here today.

"There were many Presbyteries that did not bother to create Overture 141 types of groups. Some say that we did well because we crossed prebytery lines, covered the area of four presbyteries and had active multi-ethnic groups. If it works, why can't other regions do likewise?

"I think we have demonstrated a good model of the ECC in Sierra Mission Partnership."

Cecelia Moran: ECC Charter Member and an elementary school principal in Stockton, CA

Conclusion

The 30th anniversary celebration of ECC provided a wonderful, unique opportunity to remember out roots and our faith journey, to listen to the charter members and remember those who are no longer among us, and to renew camaraderie among present ECC members. As Bryce Little put it,

> We are discovering who we are as ethnic persons and renewing our vision as to who we can become. Each of us has different functions and responsibilities, different cultural heritage and different gifts, according to the grace given to us. Each of us brings different gifts to each other and to the community. We are many. We are individuals, but still we are members together of the one body of Christ.

13. California governor Ronald Reagan's letter of commendation

RONALD REAGAN
GOVERNOR

State of California
GOVERNOR'S OFFICE
SACRAMENTO 95814

November 21, 1973

Luke I. C. Kim, M.D.
Department of Corrections
714 P Street
Sacramento, California 95814

Dear Dr. Kim:

I am enclosing a copy of correspondence I recently received commending your performance as a state employee.

May I add my thanks to those of the writer. The services you render are greatly appreciated by those of us who have the pleasure of working with you in state government.

Sincerely,

RONALD REAGAN
Governor